West of Wind

A Tribute to the West of Holsworthy

David Axtell

ARTHUR H. STOCKWELL LTD
Torrs Park   Ilfracombe   Devon
Established 1898
www.ahstockwell.co.uk

British Library Cataloguing-in-Publication Data.
A catalogue record for this book is available
from the British Library.

Arthur H. Stockwell Ltd bears no responsibility
for the accuracy of information recorded in this book.

By the same author:

Birds for All Seasons

ISBN 978-0-7223-3921-3
Printed in Great Britain by
Arthur H. Stockwell Ltd
Torrs Park   Ilfracombe
Devon

To my wife and family

Contents

List of Photographs

The Photographs 1, 4, 5, 7, 8, 11, 12 and 16 and the one on the back cover were provided by the Holsworthy Museum as were the images for the prints on the front cover and the title page; the threshing scene in Canada was supplied by The Western Producer; the rest are the author's own or were lent by relatives; those of Aston Clinton are from the Buckinghamshire County Museum collections.

Foreword

It is a great honour to be asked to write a foreword to David Axtell's book. *West of Windmill Hill* is an iconic book on Holsworthy as seen through the eyes of someone growing up in a market town in a world which was to change beyond recognition. We have a shared experience in that our childhoods and formative years were spent in Holsworthy.

I was brought up on the family farm at Holsworthy Beacon, a couple of miles away, at a time when we still had horses on the farm. The fond memories of those gentle giants, Lion and Gamespur – leading them at the end of a long day in the harvest field to Rogers Meadow, where for generations our horses had grazed through the summer months, and, in the falling dusk, watching them roll and roll in the dewy grass to rid their coats of the sweat and flies of harvest!

However, I really looked forward to going into town to meet my friends. It was like acting out for real the chapters of Richmal Crompton's *Just William*. We formed ourselves into gangs – not to terrorize the community but for adventure in the old prisoner of war camp at North Road or for damming the river at Lamerton Bridge. It was a time of freedom when our parents had complete confidence that we would come to no harm, other than the odd bruise from falling from a tree or getting wet and muddy from falling in the river catching minnows. Another attraction of town was that it had mains electricity. Incredible as it seems today, for the first eighteen years of my life we relied on oil lamps – 'tilley lights' bought at Whitlock's the ironmongers – and my granny used to complain that the light was so bright that it

9

showed up all the dust.

In Holsworthy one could open the window on the wider world at the cinema and through television. What happy hours were spent at the Tudor Cinema, at the first house on a Saturday night, when our heroes like John Wayne and James Stewart always saw that good triumphed over evil! I can still remember coming out to find a queue stretching right back to the Chapel in Bodmin Street; many had ridden their bikes from the farms of Ashwater and Halwill for a special night at the cinema. There was the final treat of sixpence worth of chips at Claude Shobbrooks before one faced the daunting ride home to Cranbury, all alone in the dark, on a bike with lights that went out every time you hit a bump.

Then, of course, the abiding memory of the 1953 Cup Final, watched at my school friend's home of Westbourne in Bodmin Street. The sitting room was filled with high excitement as the drama of the famous Stanley Matthews final unfolded live before our eyes.

However, there are direct links between the 1950s and the Holsworthy of today. The Memorial Hall opened in the fifties after an effort, in terms of fund-raising, spanning more than a generation. Just last year the hall was reopened after major renovation and it is now one of the most splendid public halls in Devon. It took twelve years to deliver, with many difficulties and heartaches along the way.

The cinema, like many country cinemas, eventually closed but in the early seventies Holsworthy Amateur Theatre Society (HATS) bought it and turned it into one of the finest theatres you can find in a small country town. It is still highly successful in terms of top quality productions and has contributed greatly to the quality of life in this deeply rural area.

Our cattle market, which is the very heartbeat of our town, is still one of the most important markets in the country. I cannot recall an occasion, as a child, when my granddad and gran ever missed market. They went for the day – dinner and tea at Sanders Café (formerly Carthew's) or the South Western Hotel. It was a time to meet your relations, neighbours and friends, to discuss the issues of the day and to catch up on the latest gossip.

St. Peter's Fair was the most important date on the calendar. It was the day you wore your Sunday best and you settled your accounts, sometimes for the whole year, with the merchants. On that day Thomas Oke & Son would bank the largest amount for the year. On the farm it was important to get the hay harvest finished before Fair so that, as Granddad used to say, 'us can enjoy fair with a good heart'.

I remember particularly the spectacle of the gypsy wedding, the fairground on a Saturday night packed to bursting point and the boxing booth where, displaying huge valour, local lads took on the booth boxers over three rounds for a fiver.

Standing out clearly in my memory also are those firms which contributed so greatly to the economic life of our town – Thomas Oke, West Devon Farmers, Whitlock's, J.E. Stacey. With the exception of the last, all have disappeared, some to be replaced by others. J.P. Whitlock, however, could never be replaced. Under one roof you could buy anything from a Ford car or tractor to a bag of nails.

When electricity arrived at Cranbury in 1959, my dad went to Whitlock's and ordered a new television. We could hardly contain our excitement (my brother Graham nearly made himself ill). The switch-on was at 7.00 p.m. – the magic of the Tudor Cinema at our remote Devon farm! Our poor old cat was so shocked by it all he hid behind the settee for two days!

It all seems a long time ago but these are treasured memories. David and I may have different memories but we share a common bond – a love of Holsworthy.

You can go away for years, but the town will always call you back. As someone who had been overseas for many years said to me, on returning to Holsworthy and feeling the thrill of seeing the church tower of St. Peter and St. Paul standing there dominating the landscape as it has done for generations, 'I knew then that I was home'.

Holsworthy has always made welcome those who have moved to our town. Many have contributed greatly to the life of the town, like David's father Eric through his business and the part he played in the life of the community. Long may that welcome continue for we need to harness the talents of all, as we in Holsworthy face the challenges of the twenty-first century. The town faces profound change and we need a new cattle market to secure our economic future. We will get there!

Maybe the Memorial Hall is a reflection of our confidence in the future. The new hall came out of the smoke and fire and heartache of foot-and-mouth and is an expression of confidence in the future. Rightly, Holsworthy wants the best!

Councillor Des Shadrick

Introduction

In this tribute to the country town in which I spent my childhood I have drawn on my own memories and on those, reaching back over a hundred years, of my grandmother, my mother, my father, who came from elsewhere to make his home here, other relatives and other Holsworthy residents.

In so doing I have tried to place the town in the broader context of its surrounding villages. My father's experiences of village life in Buckinghamshire before the First World War and of farming on the Canadian prairie, and descriptions of my schooldays in Devon and Cornwall, will, I hope, not seem out of place in the still broader context of our past English culture.

This is not an attempt to paint an overall picture of the town and its people, which has already been done by others better qualified to do so. On the other hand I hope this personal account, which gratefully acknowledges a debt to a town which allowed one of its sons to have a very small part in its affairs, will contribute to the effort to preserve Holsworthy's traditions and maintain its distinctive character as it continues to evolve.

If nothing else, I shall be satisfied if I have managed to recreate something of the atmosphere of earlier times and to stir the memories of those still living in the town or linked with its past.

The Ancient Tree and Elm Tree House

Chapter 1

An Ancient Elm

My early childhood was spent almost without interruption beyond the reach of dual carriageways in a small town and its surrounding green hills and winding lanes.

The town is itself on a hill in West Devon only a few miles from where the Atlantic breaks against the rocks of the North Cornish coast. To the east the sun rises over the top of the adjoining Windmill Hill to look down on a jumble of houses and gardens and a church tower of granite which thrusts itself towards the sky above the tops of the horse chestnuts and beeches in the churchyard. Running southwards, on either side of the hill, are two small rivers, the Deer and its tributary, which come together to the south-west of the town at Derriton and flow with combined strength towards the Tamar.

For those interested in the past, the market town of Holsworthy apparently grew from a Saxon settlement, comprising a single street with a 'Great Tree' at one end, the earl's house at the other, and the serfs' cottages on either side. An inscribed slate at the end of Fore Street commemorates an ancient elm, still remembered by some who were alive during the late forties and early fifties, the time of my early childhood. This is also where the original tree, under which the earls had dispensed justice, once stood. At the other end of Fore Street stands a group of inns named after royal emblems – the King's Arms, the Crown and Sceptre and the White Hart – the last being that of Richard II. Here, we may assume, stood the earl's house, on a site later occupied by a royal manor. Sections of the manor were leased to innkeepers – hence the royal signs.

Domesday Book records that in the reign of Edward the Confessor a manor called *Haldeurdi* with an area of 2,610 acres belonged to Harold, who had succeeded his father as Earl of the West Saxons in 1053 and later became King of England, until his defeat at the Battle of Hastings.

Haldeurdi eventually became Holsworthy, 'worthy' meaning an enclosed settlement or farm. Still pronounced 'Holsery' by many locally, the town is surrounded by many other '-worthys' in this area of West Devon and North Cornwall – Bradworthy, Pyworthy, Bulkworthy, Ugworthy, Woolfardisworthy (Woolsery), Goldsworthy, Wilworthy, Clapworthy – towns, villages, hamlets, manors and farms, some also giving their names to road crossings, such as Silworthy Cross.

On approaching Holsworthy visitors are welcomed by a sign informing them they are about to enter a Port Town. 'Port' in this context is usually taken to mean a walled or enclosed town, providing safe 'harbourage' for travellers and their goods rather than ships. There is, as far as I know, however, no archaeological evidence of stone walls as such and 'port' may be a reference to a market, in accordance with another dictionary definition of the word. The town still has a portreeve, perhaps the oldest judicial office in the country, who presides over an annual meeting of the Court Leet at which humorous petitions are now presented, observed by around three hundred spectators. After this, Ale Tasters perform their enviable task in the local inns, dating back to the time when they were appointed yearly by the Court Leet to examine, among other things, the wholesomeness of the ale.

During my childhood there were only about a thousand people living in the main part of the town and I knew at least the faces of most of them. Many had names of Devon or Cornish origin. For some, journeys of more than about fifty miles were rare and a few of the older inhabitants had visited Exeter but once or twice during their lifetimes. It was a world which had changed less in the first half of the twentieth century than it has since under the influences of road transport, television and, more recently, computers. A child grew up in a world to which it felt it belonged and became only gradually aware of things beyond. Because people travelled less, towns had more of a local character, and, in this area, the roots of that character have been traced by some to a blend of Celtic imagination tending to wildness and Saxon calm and practicality.

Records show that there was an annual fair in existence in Holsworthy as early as 1262 and a description of a weekly market first appears in 1274. A proclamation read by the town crier on the site of the ancient tree on the first day of the fair, in modern times represented by an itinerant fair company with its stalls and rides, states that the rights for a fair to be held on St. Peter's Day were granted by Henry II. On the morning of the opening of the fair each year, a Pretty Maid, selected for her 'good looks, quietness and church attendance', is revealed each year to an expectant crowd when she emerges from the church through the belfry door to receive a sum of money from the rector. The ceremony began in Victorian times when a local rector donated government stock to a trust which then yielded three pounds ten shillings annually. The first market day after Christmas is known as 'Giglets'. The dictionary defines 'giglet' as a giddy, romping girl and originally servant girls would be hired at this fair. My mother remembered it as being a time when many young men and women would come in from rural areas to make each other's acquaintance and perhaps set in motion the first steps towards marriage.

The long market square narrows at one end and then opens out into the small Stanhope Square, on one corner of which stood my grandfather's grocery and confectionery shop and next to it his café, Carthew's Corner Café. Across the road and a few yards from the site of the ancient tree after which it is named, stands Elm Tree House, to which my grandparents had moved by the time of my childhood after previously living over their business premises. Directly across Stanhope Square from Elm Tree House is Barclay's Bank, occupying a building which has changed little over the years and which reminds us of its former grandeur as a Victorian coaching inn, with a cobbled carriage stand in front.

One of the roads out of town passes the church in a curve along the wall and raised walkway which skirt the graveyard. Horses and ponies, brought in from a wide area, stood for sale here and further along the road at the time of the annual fair, until the late thirties. North Road, as it is called, then runs straight down a gentle hill, passing a row of cottages and a farm on its right. The cottages, dated 1607, were originally built of thatch and cob and the farm, belonging to Mr. Edwin Kivell and boasting a fine Georgian house, once stood on the edge of the town. At the bottom of the hill is a crossroads where North Road meets the other main route running through Holsworthy. This other road rises steeply from where it crosses the Deer's tributary to the east and falls more gradually as Sanders Lane, between tall hedges topped with trees, on the other side of the crossroads, eventually crossing the Deer itself on its way to Bude on the Cornish coast.

Opposite the church are the so-called Manor Grounds, now a car park, which accommodate the annual fair. Here may be seen the Memorial Hall, built after the war but recently given a very thorough renovation. On the east side of The Square stands the Victorian Market Hall, bisected by a covered passageway through to Fore Street. The Lower Hall was traditionally used as a meat market while the pannier market, selling produce such as eggs, vegetables and dairy products, was formerly held in the Upper Hall.

As a child I loved returning to my home town by train after a day in Exeter. After changing stations twice, once at Okehampton and once at Halwill Junction, I felt an increasing sense of remoteness and peace. On the final straight run into the station the train crossed a viaduct and I would look down to the tributary of the Deer flowing below, or ahead to my right to the random collection of buildings, including a former chapel then used to store coal, and further to the right at the top of the hill the church tower with its rookery.

In the summer we sometimes used to go to Bude by train for a day on the beach. I remember waiting on the platform for the first puff of smoke above Windmill Hill and seconds later catching sight of the front of the engine. The signalman, Mr. Jones, would then appear on the platform and, before the train stopped, he and the fireman would extend a free arm and exchange signal tokens which were in a leather pouch on the end of a steel hoop. Before the railways came, Holsworthy had been connected to Bude by a canal which was used mainly for transporting sand to improve the heavy clay soil of the district. In my grandparents' day a walk around the canal was a regular occupation on Sunday afternoons, everyone dressed in 'Sunday best' and the men carrying their favourite walking stick.

I sometimes used to sit on Market Day on the window seat in the bay of the breakfast room at Elm Tree House and look out on the square to watch the people, especially people from farms and other country folk who had come into town to do business, shop or just to have a chat. On one occasion, before I had noticed anybody cross the road, the front door opened and closed, a tap was heard at the breakfast room door and a smiling face appeared.

'Mr. and Mrs. Cathoo?' An elderly couple entered and met the welcoming gaze of my grandparents.

'You're proper strangers,' said my grandmother.

'We can't stay long. How've you been keeping, then?' They introduced a third person and then, turning to me, asked, 'Who's this young man then?' A brief exchange of news ensued after which they politely turned down an invitation to a cup of tea and departed.

Carthew is a Cornish name and my grandfather was brought up just on the other side of the Tamar in Bridgerule. I have vague memories of being told of one great-grandfather (or was it his father before him?) having won several top hats for Cornish wrestling. Among my great-grandfather Carthew's nine children were four sons. In the hope of interesting at least one of them in farming he sold his grocery business, then in Whitstone, and bought a small farm. Each of them left in turn, however, and all but my grandfather went to live in Birmingham, two becoming tailors and one a baker.

My grandfather, with an ambition of becoming an engine driver, took a steamship, the *Jelunga*, with the British India Steam Navigation Company, from London to Australia in March, 1892. He took a number

The beginning of 'Carthew's Corner'

of jobs in Queensland and later went to Melbourne. He worked on the railways but not as an engine driver. After what he later referred to as some of the best years of his life he returned and took over a post office in Plymouth for a couple of years, with one of his sisters acting as his housekeeper, before joining his widowed mother in running the grocery business in Holsworthy which his father had bought in the intervening years. He married my grandmother in 1906 and they took over the business, living in the rooms over the shop where they raised eight children. He also ran a butter and egg business, collecting from farms and delivering to shops in Torquay and to Exeter Market. He travelled by train with baskets – later a barrow – and eventually had a car. In time he rebuilt the business premises and added the café.

Elm Tree House, to which my grandparents moved when most of their children had grown up, is described by someone born there in the middle of the nineteenth century as being as far as he knew the oldest house in Holsworthy, stating that, in the reign of Queen Elizabeth, it was an inn called the Red Lion. This was the badge of the once powerful John of Gaunt who owned the manor in the fourteenth century. Cob has recently been discovered lying under some of its plaster and other clues about its past were provided by the remains of a courtyard and stables, a cellar with steps rising to the entrance of a large dining room, a set of pewter plates belonging to the house and a narrow whip cupboard fitted into one corner of the slate-floored passageway connecting the hall with the kitchen.

It was a second home to me. I was free to come and go, play a few chords on the harmonium, explore the attic or wander through the garden. My grandfather was a strongly built man with thick, white hair, kind, observant eyes and a stiff, brush-like moustache. In his later years he was unable to walk without the aid of two sticks and during winter afternoons he would sit by the fire in the breakfast room and occasionally poke it with one of his sticks or quicken the flames with a pair of bellows. For my benefit he would recite:

21

Jeremiah, blow the fire, puff, puff, puff,
First you blow it gently, then you blow it rough.
Jeremiah, blow the fire, puff, puff, puff.

In his pocket there was always a penknife and a bag of peppermints. An atmosphere of calm pervaded the room, augmented by the flicker of the fire-glow on the brass fender, the measured tick of the chiming clock on the mantelpiece and the gentle click of the brass fitting on the heavy door if someone entered or left the room. The mahogany harmonium stood in one corner, complete with mirror, brass candleholders and a seat which opened at the top for storing hymn books and psalters. My grandfather was able to take 'the organ', as it was called, to pieces to clean it. The Methodist Church once borrowed it to accompany the congregation while their organ was being repaired. Along one wall hung photographs of my mother's and my aunts' weddings, taken in the garden which my grandfather had owned at the end of Fry Street, on the opposite side of Stanhope Square from the café. Some photographs were taken in front of one of the two large greenhouses and Windmill Hill provided a perfect backdrop from this garden. Mr. Hannaford, the photographer, was a perfectionist and would take up to half an hour to set up a group. On another wall there was a picture of one of my uncles, a talented footballer and cricketer, walking out of the pavilion at the county ground to bat for Devon.

The grounds of Elm Tree House seemed enormous to me. A small garden with a lawn, bordered on two sides by the house, led via an archway into a large kitchen garden, with beds edged with box, providing flowers and vegetables. At the bottom was a stone wall, overlooking the road several feet below which ran down to the railway station. To the left of a porch in the bottom right-hand corner stood a well which my grandmother told me was never known to have gone dry and which had once supplied the nearby cottages. Beyond the porch was a large and completely private garden, along one side of which ran a high wall where my grandfather trained pears and apples; then came a sunken lawn, sometimes used for tennis, and after this an orchard. A large beech tree of considerable age stood in one corner of the sunken lawn. It was while sitting under this tree that Samuel Sebastian Wesley, composer and cathedral organist and grandson of Charles Wesley, the joint-founder of Methodism, was inspired, on hearing the church bells, to write his famous air *The Holsworthy Church Bells*.

My grandfather holding his daughter Clarice who would later run the shop

Chapter 2

My Grandmother Remembers

In her latter years my grandmother, who lived until the age of ninety-four and survived my grandfather by over twenty years, would spend every morning in a chair by the window in a corner of the kitchen at Elm Tree House. By then she was suffering from Paget's disease – a softening of the bones which had especially affected her hips, her movements being therefore restricted. She hated not being able to move about freely and probably looked back with longing to the years when she used to travel weekly by train to buy flowers at Exeter Market for making into wreaths, calling in for tea with her sister, who, with her husband, ran the North Devon Inn, before coming home. In this part of Elm Tree House she could be in touch with the day's activities – the daily help watching over the Aga or washing a few dishes, the grocer's boy arriving on an errand from the shop or the gardener passing through on his way to the garden. Here, also, she could receive her callers, who entered by a door which still opened directly on to the pavement of Bodmin Street. For many years now she had shared Elm Tree House with her eldest daughter, Clarice, who had worked at the shop since the age of fifteen and managed it for another twenty-three years after the death of my grandfather. A part of the house had eventually been sold and become a separate dwelling for a local family who had also taken over most of the garden. The wife popped in frequently to keep an eye on my grandmother and she always made her laugh as she related a piece of topical news. She had a remarkable talent for creating a picture and narrated her tale good-humouredly with a twinkle in her eye.

Apart from members of her family, other callers might include Mrs. Ben Oke, popping across for a break from the stationer, newsagent and bookshop of that name in Fore Street or Mrs. Blackshaw, smiling with strikingly dark eyes, who might snatch a moment from running her hairdressing salon across the road in Chapel Street. She had been a leading member of the Holsworthy Dramatic Society and helped in the early productions of the Holsworthy Amateur Theatre Society (HATS) which still performs in what used to be the cinema. On one occasion when I was there, a cheerful evangelist healer dropped by and I remember a more distant relative from the country, bringing with her a bunch of cottage garden flowers. Sitting next to her at the long wooden table, which extended the entire length of the window overlooking the street, I used to ask her about her childhood while we drank tea and ate saffron buns.

My grandmother was born in 1884 into a large family which lived four miles to the east of Holsworthy in the village of Halwill. I have visited the old part of the parish where they lived beside a quiet road next to the church and opposite the entrance to the manor. The only other buildings in the immediate surroundings in my grandmother's time were the village school, on the other side of the church, and the stables situated behind their house together with two other houses. Her father, Samuel Parsons, did not wish to stay on his father's farm and was much happier after he became head groom at Halwill Manor, working alongside a second groom and a stable boy. One of my grandmother's elder brothers helped at the stables and, as a young man, he would go hunting with the 'gentry'. The rest of the children used to go to the top of the church tower and watch the hounds running.

Living at the manor was Squire Harris, who had begun life in Stoke Newington in London and had become a corn merchant. From there he moved to Kent and then to West London, presumably as his fortunes improved, before taking the manor at Halwill. He carried a walking stick, and, when in a bad mood, would walk with his hands behind his back, trailing it. Apart from the grooms, he also employed a cook, a

Halwill Manor

kitchen maid, a second kitchen maid, an all-purpose tweeny maid, two housemaids, head and second, a parlourmaid, a lady's maid, a butler, an under-butler and gardeners. The people in the village did not feel at all inferior to those at the manor and were not jealous of them. The 'gentry' dressed for dinner in the evening at the manor – the women in long gowns and the men in tails – and, when there was a dance, the windows were left wide open and the curtains drawn back. The village children were allowed to watch the guests dancing to early gramophone records from outside. 'We used to think it was wonderful,' my grandmother said. Squire Harris looked after his staff well. He always called my grandmother by both of her Christian names, Ada Mary. Once, when she was looking pale he sent his butler over with a bottle of port, and at Christmas the family would always receive a case of wine.

My grandmother's mother, Norah Ellen, was one of the daughters of a 'yeoman farmer' at Milton Damerel, James Moore, and, like all of her sisters, had been privately educated and was expected to marry a substantial farmer. Her father, therefore, did not at first approve of her future husband, whom she had met while staying on a farm in Halwill during harvesting. She was fond of writing verses, a poem of hers, entitled *Happiness*, appearing in the local paper at the time of her diamond wedding anniversary. It contains the lines:

> By doing good to others, we gain a happy mind,
> We must learn to part from trouble and leave it far behind.

A visitor, on passing the village schoolroom in those days by foot, horse or horse and cart, might have heard the sound of children singing or reciting verses, which my grandmother could still recite word-perfect in her old age:

> I wish I lived in a caravan,
> With a horse to drive, like a pedlar man!
> Where he comes from nobody knows,
> Or where he goes to, but on he goes! . . .

or:

> High in the belfry the old sexton stands,
> Grasping the rope with his thin, bony hands . . .

or perhaps:

> The fire brigade is a famous host,
> Ever ready, ever steady, pumping away . . .

A game they played in the school playground was 'jump-back'. One child would stand facing the wall and another would climb on to his or her back. One by one the other children would jump on to see how many could stay on at the same time.

When not at school, my grandmother took her turn to feed maize to the hens which ran about the stable yard. In the cold winters of those days the ponds froze over every year and the children regularly skated. The girls used to skip a lot, two holding the end of the long rope and four or five skipping at the same time. One of the favourite occupations of the boys was marbles, which would be set up in a large circle with the ally in the middle. There was always a swing fixed up and my grandmother's brothers made their own stilts. They also made their own kites and sometimes a pig's bladder was inflated to serve as a ball. Not all families could afford a bicycle and my grandmother's brothers shared one between them. Indoors the children could play dominoes, ludo or snap but they were not allowed to have ordinary playing cards. My great-grandparents were keen draughts players and there was one sure way of knowing how the game was going – if they had to shut the door when they came into the room, mother was losing! On Sundays my great-grandmother would sit and talk quietly with her best friends in the parlour, the children not being allowed in, although they could peer around the door. While indoors they always had to be on their best behaviour or they were sent out on to the lawn to play.

Weekly chores had to be performed without the modern conveniences which we now take for granted but there was plenty of help at hand.

The copper for washing clothes was filled with water and stood over a fire every Monday before the arrival of the washerwoman. Every home had a knife-board and knife-powder for use on 'knife-cleaning day'. Most of the baking was, of course, done at home. Fresh meat – beef or lamb – was eaten only once a week when the butcher came around. In the pantry, there was a salter where bacon and hams were left soaking in brine and then hung. For making cream, fresh milk was first stood in large pans for a few hours for the cream to rise. It was then scalded on a stove where the thick, yellow crust gradually formed. When a ring of milk appeared around the edge it was taken away and placed on cold stone slabs to cool. Later the cream was removed with a skimmer. Each farm made its own butter, the farmer's wife simply stirring and beating the cream by hand.

In those days women's dresses were long so they used to gather mud and clothes generally were brushed more than washed – 'There were always heaps of brushes about,' my grandmother told me. As well as having special clothes for Sunday, everybody had a pair of Sunday boots which were cleaned on Mondays and put on one side for the following Sunday. My great-grandmother used to knit stockings for the girls and socks for the boys and men, and sewing women would come to stay for ten days or so and work through the pile of accumulated mending.

My grandmother liked children and was nursemaid to her younger sisters as was so often the case in large families. On one of her birthdays she collected several children of only three or four years old from local families and gave them a special afternoon, with lots of games and treats, before taking them home again. She also liked animals and surprised her mother by one day bringing a visitor's horse into the kitchen. She very much enjoyed walking. It was mile or two to the village shop, where she could buy plenty of sweets for one penny, and a four mile walk each way to her music lesson. She would cut across the fields and, if she passed through one with turnips, would select a small, fresh, white one to eat. She often walked three or four miles collecting money from houses for missions. Walking provided many pleasures – there were more byways, many more wild flowers and butterflies and more wild strawberries than today. It was not uncommon to meet a tramp but nobody feared any harm from strangers.

Once a year my great-grandmother would take the family on a 'blackberry picnic' on Cookbury Moor. This was before it was planted with conifers (something which always made my grandmother 'mad' when she thought about it). They would take rolls, small pasties, freshly baked cakes and splits with jam and cream. My great-grandmother also arranged the local cricket teas, there being a team in every village then. Tables and forms were set up in the corner of the field, hot water was brought in a copper kettle from the boiler in the pavilion and no one went hungry. Sometimes in the evenings, at home or in the schoolroom, there were magic-lantern shows – photographs of buildings or famous places, perhaps – projected on to a screen. For holidays my grandmother stayed on the farms of relatives, travelling by horse and carriage. She remembered the first 'jingles' – known as governess carts in other parts of the country – light two-wheeled vehicles with seats at the side and easy access from the rear. On one journey she threw a couple of oranges she happened to have with her to a stone-cracker, as he knelt splitting stones beside the road; on another she passed a steamroller, preceded by a man with a red flag. When staying on a farm near Tavistock she used to walk on to Dartmoor to pick whortleberries, more commonly known now as bilberries.

As she grew older she played the organ regularly on Sundays at Stowford Chapel, a mile's walk away. She also played each week at choir practice at Muckworthy Chapel, as well as at Halwill Church, where her father, Samuel Parsons, was choirmaster. At one chapel anniversary tea the minister, relying on her familiarity with the services, said 'Miss Parsons, will you raise the doxology?' She sang 'Praise God, from Whom all blessings flow' all the way through and nobody joined in. It was only afterwards that she remembered that she should have sung 'Be present at our table, Lord.' On Saturday and Sunday evenings she played the harmonium in the parlour at home and all the family would gather around and sing. She was still able to play in her

31

eighties, although this role was usually performed by her eldest daughter, Clarice, at similar family gatherings of the next generation.

At this point let us leave my grandmother for a while and describe how my father, who was not born in Devon and was, therefore, 'a foreigner', came to be there.

Brought up in the village of Aston Clinton on the northern edge of the Chilterns, in Buckinghamshire, he had left England for Canada in 1925 where he spent several months on the prairie and then a year in Vancouver. He returned to England not long after the General Strike and everywhere that he looked people were forming long queues in search of employment. It made a deep impression on him and one which remained with him all his life. He was fortunate enough to obtain a job selling fire extinguishers and became top salesman out of about one hundred and seventy. This led to a posting to Ceylon, where, in contrast to the situation he had left behind, he sampled colonial life at the legendary Mount Lavinia Hotel and dined and played bridge regularly with tea planters. After a while he moved on to northern India for a few months. On returning to England, he joined an oil company which sent him to the West Country. This he always regarded as a stroke of good fortune.

He stayed first at Two Waters Foot near the village of St. Neot with its small river flowing off Bodmin Moor. After establishing a few contacts in Cornwall, he moved to Exeter where he shared digs with the head of the English Department at Hele's School. At weekends they were joined for excursions by the games master and the music master, an amateur ornithologist. They often went out on the golf course and, while the former took his game seriously, the latter became easily distracted. After he had disappeared into the bushes to find his ball it would often be some time before he re-emerged. 'Sorry old chaps,' he said on one occasion, 'I've just been studying the feeding habits of the corn bunting.' Another day, after he had gone off somewhere for more than half an hour, they discovered him sitting on the bank of a river with manuscript and pencil. 'Just writing down the music of the stream,' he explained.

My father's journeys as a commercial traveller sometimes took him through Holsworthy, where he would always have lunch in my grandfather's café. On the first occasion it was a Wednesday and, being Market Day, the café was full. My mother was taking the money and, as my father passed her on the way out, she asked, 'Weren't you able to find a seat?', adding, 'Perhaps you will come back later.' 'Perhaps I *will*,' he replied. By the time he returned my grandfather had finished carving and had relieved her at the till so she made a point of serving him. She did so again on subsequent occasions, sometimes first going upstairs to put on a string of beads.

As he grew to know my mother better my father's visits to Holsworthy became more frequent and he would sometimes stay overnight at Elm Tree House. He thus became more acquainted with my grandfather and recalls his protesting one morning, 'What do you think of it, Eric? There's three middens running about here and my boots haven't been cleaned!' My father would sometimes accompany my grandfather on his country rounds or visits to an auction sale. On one such occasion, my grandfather, in need of directions, drew up beside two country women who were all of forty and suggested, 'Let's ask these two middens!' On another, it was a fine day and the furniture was out in the open. My grandfather sat down in an armchair, made himself comfortable, took out his pocket knife, and began paring his nails. 'Come on now, George,' said the auctioneer, 'we want to sell that one.'

My father would have considered buying a farm but knew he would have had little success in trying to persuade my mother to agree to it. Her ideas about local farming were probably coloured by what she had been told of past conditions for some:

Farmers going to bed in their day shirts and long underpants, leaving ice-cold parlours in winter for bedrooms with floors covered with oilcloth or with no covering at all, and some of them wrapping a heated brick in flannel to warm the bed; sheds being of galvanised iron and cows sometimes having to stand in a foot or more of mud when milked – the worst of the dung being washed off their teats and the milk filtered though gauze; when it came to eating, the only meat for most of the year being 'risty bacon', as they called it.

This was possibly a somewhat distorted picture but as far as meat consumption was concerned it had been true that many farmers kept two pigs for a year, then sold one and killed the other, preserving some of the meat in salt. Beef had, for some, been a luxury enjoyed only on such occasions as Harvest Sunday or Christmas. Although things had improved considerably, all this hearsay ensured that my mother would never contemplate being a farmer's wife. Having reached the age of twenty-one, she married my father and they moved into the bungalow, called Upcott, which was to become my home.

Chapter 3

My Father Arrives

My father did not expect to spend the rest of his life in the town of Holsworthy although, once he had arrived in the West Country, he never thought of living anywhere else. But for the war he might well have moved closer to Exeter but, as time went by, he settled permanently at Upcott and, looking back later over his life, had no regrets. By the time he married he had already done all the travelling he wanted to do and became involved with many aspects of town life.

He continued his travels for the oil company in Cornwall where the people, he discovered, are fiercely loyal if they take to you, and he liked their plain and honest way of talking. At Penzance, he was greeted from a distance of over fifty yards by a high-pitched squeal – 'Where the hell've ya bin?' The enquirer spoke with a particularly thick accent and, in the conversation which followed, my father asked 'What the hell are you talking about?' to which he replied, 'Don't 'ee understand English?' One Cornish client, on whom my father called regularly, had never failed to order a drum of oil. On one occasion he was inside his garage when my father arrived and, wandering in, he discovered about ten barrels stacked up at the back, about two years' supply for his single lorry. 'Why do you keep ordering when you've got this lot to get rid of?' he asked. 'I don't like to send 'ee off with nothing when 'ee've come all this way,' the man explained.

My father called one evening at the house of another customer, a thin old Cornishman of about six feet in height, in a bowler hat and collarless shirt, and, entering a room, he found himself confronted by nineteen girls and boys sitting quietly on benches against each of the walls.

'Hello!' he said, 'are you all having a party?'

'No sir,' the man replied, 'they be all my own.'

'How did you manage that?' asked my father, noticing the eldest was only about fourteen years old.

'Well, sir,' the man said, 'some is twins. You be a twin ben 'ee m'dear,' he added, looking at one little girl.

'No, father,' she replied, 'It's 'er and 'er and 'im and 'er!' she said, pointing around the room.

A few months later my father arrived with nineteen oranges and packets of wine gums and asked how the children were progressing.

'Oh! We've made it up to a score, sir!' said the man. 'Missus, bring out the new baby for the gentleman to see!'

After living abroad my father was glad to be back in England and, apart from loving the landscape of Devon and Cornwall, he probably felt at home there because there had been less change than in the county of his birth. All through his life part of my father belonged to another age. He clung to memories of his childhood in the tranquil setting of rural England before the First World War changed the world for ever. This desire not to forget the past, and a belief that the examples of the past provide clues on how to find happiness and fulfilment in our lives, is perhaps something I have inherited and a reason for my writing things down.

He was born in 1900, a few months before the death of Queen Victoria, in the village of Aston Clinton. This lies in the Chilterns between Tring to the south and, to the north, the county town of Aylesbury, which had already begun to expand rapidly. The main road through the village was the Roman Akeman Street and was crossed by the ancient Icknield Way. Most of the village employment was provided by the Rothschilds, of banking renown. Sir Anthony's widow owned the mansion and estate at Aston Clinton at this time and nearby Halton was the larger estate of Alfred de Rothschild.

My grandfather was Lady de Rothschild's under-butler. He was quiet and gentle and always brought a small gift for my father at the end of the day – an apple, a sweet or a biscuit. After the evening meal he would sometimes build up a stack of sovereigns in his hand and, as he was about to close it, would tell my father he could keep any he could grab first. He was never able to do so, so one day knocked his hand from below and scattered the coins all over the floor. He remembered his father taking part in a donkey race and Lady de Rothschild shouting 'Come *on*, Axtell!' He would probably have become head butler but, one spring, he took a favourite walk along the Aylesbury arm of the Grand Union Canal, and, after pausing to fill his pipe by one of the locks, fainted, fell into the canal and drowned. It appears that he had not been feeling well for quite some time. He was only thirty-four and my grandmother was left to bring up my father, aged nine, and his two elder sisters, on her own. My father used to paint in words a forlorn picture of his widowed mother, his two sisters and himself, waiting in the rain at a hamlet called World's End to be picked up for a journey to Princes Risborough in an uncle's horse-drawn baker's van. They stood under a chestnut tree, the rain soaking through their clothes and the black dye from his cap running down his face.

All this was a far cry from my mother's upbringing with her five sisters and two brothers in the rooms above the shop and café in Holsworthy. They knew little of privacy, sleeping two or three in one bed. By the same token they never lacked companions. All the girls, except one whom my grandparents were able to send away to board, went daily by train to the county school in Bude. Most of the holidays were spent working in the café and, at the age of sixteen, the girls left school to work there full-time. They were considered to be a very smart family and two of them in particular went on to distinguish themselves during the war, serving overseas.

My mother was the fourth child, and being born between the two brothers tended to prefer the company of boys. She would play hopscotch or rounders with her brothers and their friends in the square, and, later, hockey or even cricket. On Wednesdays she would wait with a stick with one of her brothers and a cousin at the cemetery at the end of North Road to help a farmer called Ned Batten to drive his cattle to the market in the square, for which they would each receive a penny. Every shop used to have a railing to place across the doorway on the pavement to prevent livestock from entering. The Band of Hope, a travelling mission often remembered for preaching temperance, would arrive by van and offer a Gospel to any child who would perform a Sankey hymn such as 'I'm on the inside, which side are you?' or 'My sins are as high as a mountain'. After receiving one of each of the Gospels a child could ask for a sixpence instead. My mother and her brothers were regular performers, perhaps spending their money at a film show in the Market Hall. Sometimes, for a holiday, my mother stayed with the parents of her former nursemaid, Bessie Cole, at Week St. Mary, about ten miles away across the county border, where according to my grandmother people were said to 'speak differently' from Holsworthy people. Bessie Cole's father was the local carrier and used to bring butter, cheese, baskets of eggs, flowers and fruit to the pannier market in Holsworthy. He also carried passengers. A form was placed down the middle of his cart to provide extra seating and the rest of the passengers sat around the edge. At the bottom of a steep hill everyone except the driver would have to get out and walk to the top, where they would wait for the cart to pick them up again. At other times my mother stayed on the farm of an uncle at Sutcombe and especially enjoyed riding to chapel in his jingle.

Every Sunday during the summer the family went to the beach at Bude. My grandfather had an Armstrong Siddeley with a sliding glass panel separating the driver from the passengers. It was large enough to accommodate eight, two children sitting on biscuit tins between the partition and the rear seat. My grandmother would sit in the middle of the back seat, allowing the two boys to ride in the front. They used to make faces through the glass to start the girls laughing, much to the annoyance of my grandfather who was trying to concentrate on driving. Once, as the noise reached a pitch, the panel slid back and he roared over his shoulder, 'You're like a lot of blimmen' monkeys, and your mother's the biggest monkey of the lot', which set them off laughing again even more loudly. At one point the Bude road gradually climbs a hill and, just before reaching the summit, offers a first glimpse of the sea. Here one of the younger children might try to be the first to call out, 'I see the sea. Nobody sees it but me!' – a tradition carried forward into my own childhood.

My grandfather had answered an advertisement in the paper by the London and South Western Railway Company and bought the redundant stock of a luggage van and passenger wagon. He had arranged for them to be hauled by traction engine all the way to Bude from Okehampton. They had had to come via Kilkhampton as they were unable to make the turn at Stratton. The Bird's Nest, as it was called, stood under the shelter of a hedge at the top of a hill on the edge of the downs to the north of Crooklets beach where it became the setting for summer holidays for many years ahead. It was separated from the rest of the field by wooden fencing and a stepladder on either side of the hedge behind provided access to a short cut across the cliffs to Crooklets, the nearest beach. My grandfather was good with his hands and kept the wagons in a sound state of repair, attending to roofs, doors and interiors and repainting the outside dark green each spring. The luggage van provided ample space for a cooker and sink at one end, a long scrubbed wooden table and benches in the middle and a couch and armchairs at the other end, from where the large doorway, when opened, provided an inland view across a valley dotted with spires and steeples. The passenger wagon was divided into five bedrooms, each with the original door, with a brass handle and leather strap to open the window. Each of these had a cotton curtain which fluttered in the wind.

At Crooklets, the best beach for surfing in Bude, a collection of wooden bathing huts, each a different shape and colour, was grouped in a crescent at one corner of the bay where tough dune grass bound the sandy soil and provided the space for sitting. Concrete steps led down to pebbles at the head of the sandy beach. Proof of the arrival of emancipation is provided by snapshots of my mother and her sisters, in the fashionable swimming costumes and hats of the twenties, playing leapfrog. Sea-bathing had by then become popular although the men still often swam, as they had for many years, in Sir Thomas's Pit, a pool partly hewn out of Barrel Rock, on the edge of Bude Breakwater, by the forces of the sea. My grandmother had never become comfortable with the practice of bathing in the sea. When members of her family were in the water she would try to keep them in her line of vision and intermittently called out, 'Can anyone see so-and-so?'

My mother, who passed from serving in the café straight into marriage, used to say that she regretted never having had a little more freedom and independence. She would have liked to have studied for a qualification in domestic science and perhaps taught that subject. After less than two years of marriage, my eldest sister was born, three years later came my next sister and I appeared four years after that. My grandfather had a particular soft spot for my mother and in her early years of marriage, before he had trouble with his legs, used to walk out to Upcott every Sunday morning after chapel and place a bar of Cadbury's chocolate on the kitchen mantelpiece for her before he left.

After four years of marriage war broke out. My father's Great-aunt Isabella, a widow, came to stay for a while during the war after her house in London had been bombed. Half-buried under the rubble, she had sent the rescue party next door to help a crippled old lady, although she was over eighty herself. She was a religious soul and had donated six hundred pounds to a group of nonconformists to enable them to build a meeting room in Aston Clinton, where she had been brought up, and had also given my father a 'start in life', as he called it, so that he could put down a deposit to buy Upcott, for which he was always grateful. During the war years my father kept a cow in the field next to our house. There was a pond in the far corner which was occupied by ducks and also by numerous frogs at certain times of the year. He also kept up to one hundred and fifty chickens in the run between the back garden and the field and a couple of pigs in a shed in the corner of the yard behind the house.

One morning after a blustery March night my mother called out to

The Furry Dance at 'Carthew's Corner'

my father that there was a big, grey bird on the lawn. It was a heron which had exhausted itself in the high winds and perhaps flown into the telegraph wire overhead. My father caught it as it tried to struggle through the wire fence between the front garden and the yard. He decided to keep it for a while in the fruit frame for blackberries and raspberries in the back garden. He gave it fish waste from the café and it gradually became tame enough to feed from his hand. When 'Horace' was fully recovered he set it free but it was reluctant to go. Errand boys, arriving whistling on bicycles, would be silenced as they turned the corner to find themselves suddenly confronted by a heron standing motionless in front of the back door. Horace discovered the pond and ditch at the far side of the field and this became his hunting ground. If anybody called my father would ask if they would like to see a heron. At the call of 'Horace' a head and neck like a walking stick would slowly appear from the ditch and turn in the direction of the house. 'Come on!' my father would shout, waving a piece of fish, and the bird would rise into the air and flap across the field to land at his feet. Towards the end of the spring Horace began to fly around the house in ever-widening circles. One day he flew low over the yard, as if to say farewell, and set off in the direction of what my father hoped was his former home.

Chapter 4

After the War

Upcott is situated in North Road just past the crossroads. It was built by the local vet, Mr. William Penhale, for his retirement and named after Upcott Farm, near Cookbury to the east of Holsworthy. Penhales had been farmers and vets in that area for much longer than anybody can remember, at one time curing herbs in the chimney for treating animals. William's father, Richard, was the first vet to set himself up in Holsworthy and the practice continued to be passed down from one generation to the next. I believe that Mr. Penhale did not enjoy a long retirement at Upcott and, quite soon after he died, my father bought it, at the same time renting part of the four acres of land attached to it, later to become known as Upcott Field.

Upcott was an 'American bungalow', with windows peeping through the tiles of the roof on three sides. It stood well back from the road on a high mound, with a verandah and lawns to the front and one side and a drive going up the other side to a yard at the back. The front path was broken by two flights of steps and on each side of the higher one stood a pedestal bearing an ornamental flowerpot, usually planted with geraniums. In line with these steps, on both sides, a bank divided the front lawn into two levels. Steps from the road rose to a wooden front gate with a small pillar on either side. The cream wooden fence along the front matched another one running between the columns of the verandah, which was covered in roses. There were two flower beds to the front of the house and two along the sides of the lawns. The view from the upper lawn, or through the windows when indoors, over the heads of the passers-by, was to the fields rising from the valley to Windmill Hill.

Only a few cars drove past during the course of the day although North Road is the main road to Bideford. One Saturday morning I went down to the front fence to collect car numbers but gave up after only managing to write down two in an hour and spending most of my time watching tiny red spiders running in and out of the cracks of the wooden crossbars.

People more than cars went by and their faces became familiar. There was a man in a cap and pale brown dealer's coat, pushing a bicycle laden with hay, who regularly opened and disappeared through a mysterious door in the hedge on the other side of the road. Many years later I learnt that he was called Reg Davey and used to come out daily to feed horses there. He would also pass by later with a bucket over the handlebars of the bicycle to attend to calves in a field on the edge of the town. Here he would sit and enjoy a quiet rest with a cigarette before returning. There was a painter and decorator, Mr. Paddison, with his checked cap and pencil moustache, whistling and giving me a friendly nod as he cycled past and a dignified lady in an elegant hat, as befits the wife of the proprietor of Oke's The House of Fashion, returning to her house set well back from the road with large bay windows. There was the odd person going to and from the houses which stood on the far side of our field, converted from huts built to house Italian prisoners of war, and finally there was the cross-bearer at church services, Mr. Taylor, who would stop for a chat and to admire the roses on the verandah.

Mr. Paddison, son of a blacksmith, bred pigeons for racing and at the suggestion of a Mr. 'Lew' Edwards, who was breeding a lot of them for use in the war, had transferred to the Pigeon Corps. He was also an expert on bees and travelled all over the county setting up hives.

This was where my parents set up house together and raised three children. The war was almost over by the time I was born but as I grew older I started to become aware of its aftermath, including the strain it had been on my mother. Her work as a mother and housewife was increased by the addition of evacuee children – six altogether who lived with us at various times. There were gas masks lying about in cupboards and I came across blackout material – my mother was reluctant to throw away anything which might come in useful. My sisters still had some wooden toys which had been carved by the Italian prisoners of war. Of course there were ration books and children were entitled to free bottles of orange juice, which I seem to remember had blue labels, from the Food Office. There was still a feeling of unease when planes flew over and my sisters would run indoors. German planes had come over Holsworthy during the war but the only bomb which had fallen came down in a field at Sutcombe, a few miles away, killing two cows. Sometimes, when I looked across at Windmill Hill from the lawn, I saw men walking around the square building which breaks the skyline roughly where the windmill had stood until around 1890, and imagined them to be German spies. I have since learnt that this was a Royal Observer Corps post and that it continued to operate for a long while after the war had ended.

I was born two weeks after D-Day in a cottage hospital at Halwill Junction, not far from the station and about two miles from Halwill village where my grandmother had been brought up. Since it was June my mother used to wheel the pram out on to the verandah at Upcott and I like to imagine that some of my early days were spent waking in the sunshine to the scent of roses, the songs of birds and the sound of leisurely footsteps and voices from the pavement. Had I been born two weeks earlier, would I have woken to the roar of engines as planes passed over Holsworthy carrying troops to Normandy?

When I was old enough I spent a lot of my time in the yard which was surrounded on all sides, by the house, a fence and an assortment of buildings, and I felt secure from any intrusion from the outside world. Between the yard and the back garden, to the west, was the hay-shed, a square, black construction of corrugated steel, at the back of which my father stored hay and straw. In the bottom corner stood an oblong building of wood divided halfway to the roof inside by a partition over which I liked to clamber. One side of it was the woodshed where a rusty vice, fixed to the floor, leaned loosely against a wooden workbench; the other side was occupied by a sow and piglets; its outside wall was insulated by a double thickness of wooden planks and I could hear rats running to and fro, knocking their bodies against the sides. The outer layer was beginning to rot and I would break off bits of wood in my hand easily, as if the planks were made of dry biscuit. Next to this building was a green wooden garage, against which I often spent entire days kicking a rubber ball in an imaginary football match between my left and right foot, or, in summer, throwing a tennis ball and hitting it with a cricket bat on the rebound. A defunct water pump stood between the garage and the woodshed in a gap leading to the crumbling damp earth, smelling of mould and ivy, of the hedge behind. From here I would climb cautiously on to the rusty corrugated steel roof of the woodshed to pick hazelnuts, sometimes still soft, green and sweet.

One of my earliest memories of the yard was of a group of boys in boxing gloves around the area of the hay-shed. Much later, I was to learn that, shortly after the war, my father had become aware of the fact that these youths had wanted to play in football matches but were too young to join Holsworthy's adult team, the Magpies. He, therefore, formed the Scarlet Runners, which not only enjoyed considerable success but proved to be the nursery for talent about to burst forth, some of it exceptional. The Ford, Rogers and Hawkins families were among those each producing more than one of the players emerging at this time but the name which appeared most was Harris. When I was older, football matches started to be played in Upcott Field and I could watch them, without having to pay, through our fence of wire netting. Michael Harris, who played halfback, was a joy to watch. He would be an example to many a top professional were he playing today, never resorting to fouls to compensate for a lack of skill, never wasting a pass or making a careless one. He went on to play professionally for Bideford but, missing Holsworthy, returned to live here again. He was

My father with the Scarlet Runners

playing for the Magpies when they won the Devon Senior Cup, under the captaincy of centre forward Eric French, at Home Park in 1953. They were playing against Dartmouth United, which had beaten them twice in recent matches. Charlie Sleeman, at right wing, scored the winning goal. 'I was afraid to kick it (in case it went over the top) so I ran it into the net,' were his words. Eric French might have played professionally for Plymouth Argyle but he had to go off to do national service and when he returned he was just too old – the scouts of the professional sides were looking out for younger players.

The late forties was also a time when members of the parish council, churchwardens, bell-ringers under Mr. C. Lyle and the rector, mindful of the sorry state of the church bells, had decided at a meeting to have them recast with increased weight and a tenor of fifteen hundredweight. In the words of a later Steeplekeeper and Captain of the Tower, Ralph Chapman:

> I understand from the late Mr. Fred Sangwin (an authority on bells) that he was invited to attend the meeting and that he advised 'if they are going to recast, have a 15 cwt tenor and you will have a good peal'. How right he was!

The church had once had a carillon but this had ceased to function in 1910. My father suggested that installing a new carillon at the same time as a new ring of bells would encourage people to donate money. Whether this argument carried any weight with the parish council I do not know but, for whatever reason, this is what they agreed to do. One of the thirteen tunes of the new carillon would obviously be Wesley's *The Holsworthy Church Bells*, which had also been a feature of the earlier one.

Some confusion exists over when Wesley wrote this composition but it would seem likely, from the various pieces of information available, that the sequence of events was something like this. Wesley struck up a friendship with Dr. Ash, a local man whose parents had run The Tree Hotel in Stratton, at the time when he had been invited to

Holsworthy to play its organ, perhaps at the dedication service some time after its installation. Wesley, by now cathedral organist at Gloucester, stayed with the doctor at Penroses next to Elm Tree House in Bodmin Street and they apparently shared a common interest in fishing and field sports. Ash had been interested in installing a carillon and raised or donated money for this purpose. Wesley composed two tunes for it, including *The Holsworthy Church Bells* and also adapted a melody by Mozart for it. The full organ piece, *An Air Composed for Holsworthy Church Bells*, came considerably later and whether Wesley actually played this at Holsworthy or not is not certain. He certainly continued to correspond with Dr. Ash and was planning to visit his friend again. Ill health, however, prevented him from doing so and he died at the age of sixty-five. Wesley had found life trying, complaining especially about the standard of the choirs prevalent in his time and the fact that members of the clergy were nominally in charge of the organist. This was a period also when, too often, scant regard was given to music in cathedrals and those who performed it. On top of this, there was in his family a tendency towards depression, which affected him and had also affected his father. One of Wesley's sons spent half of his life in an asylum while two of them took their own lives. We may assume that the composer received some consolation from his friendship with Dr. Ash, to whom he dedicated a revised work for five-part choir and organ, *I am Thine O save me.*

My father agreed to organise the fund-raising for the bells and carillon which took place during the years 1947-49. Whether the one hundred pounds for restoring the carillon, donated by Dr. Ash to celebrate his appointment as portreeve, was still available for use is not clear. Three annual summer fairs were held in Stanhope Park, along with teas in the pavilion, evening whist drives, clay pigeon shoots and other events and many business donors were recorded.

I remember at least one of the summer fairs in the park with hoopla and home produce stalls, bowling for a pig, a maypole and the playing of the town band. One of them was opened, in response to an invitation by my father, by Joe Louis, who for some is still the greatest world heavyweight boxing champion of all time. He was already familiar with the area, having been stationed near Holsworthy during the war. He drew an enormous crowd to the park where he refereed a boxing match and made a speech. My father received a generous response to his request for contributions to the fund from a man we knew as Uncle Silas; he was an American lawyer who had founded a family organisation for those with the Axtell surname in the days when tracing ancestors was still relatively rare. One Christmas after the war he had kindly sent 'turkey dinners' to eight Axtell families in England in consideration, as he put it, of 'their sacrifice during the war, and their present suffering from socialism and austerity'. He visited us one summer when we were staying at an old caravan in Widemouth, where we used to go for our annual holiday. His pretty wife introduced my sisters and me to the concept of America's having a separate language when she referred to biscuits as 'cookies'.

The bell-ringers did not forget my father's hard work in raising the money for the bells and invited him and my mother each year to accompany them on the bell-ringers outing, on which he used buy them all an ice cream.

Many of us look back on the fifties as a time when people wanted to rebuild their lives and the home and family were central. At another time of peace in the English countryside, around 1900, my grandmother was moving forward from childhood to adulthood. As we sat chatting at the kitchen table in Elm Tree House she told me about her last years in the village of Halwill before she came to live permanently in Holsworthy. She could not remember ever having her hair cut. 'Girls' hair,' she said, 'was allowed to grow long and at fifteen you put your hair up and wore a long skirt, which you held up at one side as you walked. You were grown up then.' She wore no make-up and never wore any jewellery although every young man who could afford it carried a watch and chain.

At that time the harvest was the main event of the year. Farmers, their wives and children, and labourers all worked together and assisted neighbouring farms. All those involved in a harvest were invited to a

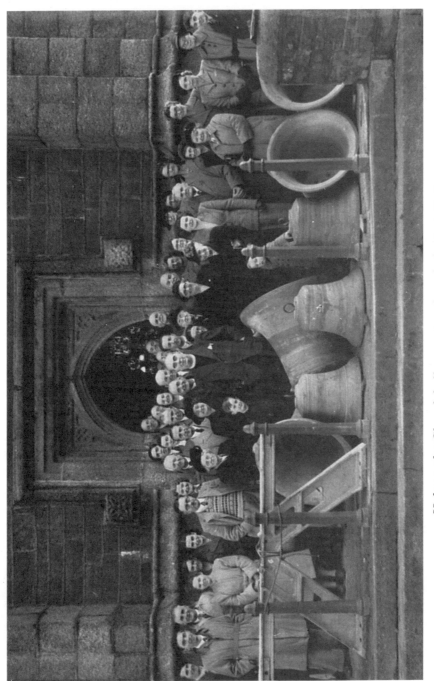

Holsworthy Church bells recast and ready for installation

supper – the harvest home. At the hay harvest the men would begin to mow around the edge of the field with scythes and, as the unmown part in the centre grew smaller, rabbits would break cover and try to reach the hedgerows before they were shot. The grass was turned, left to dry then piled up in 'pokes' and, at a later stage, a rick was built up from these. The farmer's wife always arranged for the women to take out the 'drinking' to the men – tea in cans – and they might also be given small pasties. There was a tradition of 'making the hay sweet', as it was called. In the evening some of the young men would each form a small ring from a handful of hay and chase the girls until they managed to kiss one of them through it, after which they would push the ring into the side of the haystack.

Chapel Anniversary was an important event for chapel people. After tea the young men and women used to go into the nearest field for such games as *twos-and-threes* or *kiss-in-the-ring*. For *twos-and-threes* all the men and women stood in pairs and formed a large circle except for two, one of whom would be 'he'. When the game started the other unattached person, to avoid being caught, would run and stand in front of one of the pairs. At this point the man or woman thus duplicated would have to break from the circle and try to reach another pair without being caught. For *kiss-in-the-ring* the men and women, apart from two, stood alternately in a ring holding hands and a similar chase-and-catch procedure ensued as before. If a young man felt a fancy towards a particular girl he would offer to walk her home afterwards. 'You might meet your best boyfriend this way,' my grandmother said. There were village dances but my grandmother was never allowed to go to the dances in the towns which were considered to be 'common'. Other events which she was allowed to attend, however, were flower shows, bicycle races in the fields and, at Christmas, carol singing. In her early married life she was pianist for a concert party which performed at chapels over a wide area.

At fifteen, my grandmother began her apprenticeship at a dressmaker's in Holsworthy. The shop, Lovell's, was situated in the market square and there were eight dressmakers and half a dozen tailors.

'A factory-made garment in those days was considered inferior, and referred to as "only an old ready-made thing",' my grandmother told me, adding that not only dresses but shirts, underlinen and, of course, suits were all made by hand. She was beginning to feel really grown up by now since, like all the dressmakers, who lived over the shop, she was now called 'miss', a token of respect, and she wore a black dress.

The business of Ernest Harold Lovell is listed in Kelly's Directory for 1902 as 'practical tailor, woollen and linen draper, silk mercer, dress, mantle and millinery warehouse'. This clearly defines the extent of its dramatic growth from the small tailoring concern established in Holsworthy over forty years earlier by his father, Timothy, who was born the son of a silk weaver, probably of Huguenot descent, in Bethnal Green in London.

My grandmother never received payment for her work. Whatever she was owed was deducted from her father's account. The business used to give a 'good dinner' to its main customers twice a year at which time bills were settled. If there was a special order on hand the dressmakers and milliners would sometimes work all night for no extra pay. My grandmother would sing to keep them awake in the early hours of the morning. An example of this might be a wedding, for which the bride-to-be would perhaps choose special fabrics for her dress and hat and detailed work might be involved, while for the trousseau a set of six of each item was made. Sometimes as she looked out of the window at Lovell's she would see my grandfather going to fill two cans with water from the pump in the centre of the square. She considered this to be 'dreadfully lowering' for somebody who was running his own business. Although she lived over the shop all week, she travelled back to Halwill at weekends by train to be with her family. She was often escorted to the station by my grandfather and she would be met by the booking clerk at the other end!

When talking about her father, Samuel Parsons, she related how, several years later, he moved to Holsworthy, bought the first T Ford to be sold in the town and started a car hire and taxi business there. Many years after that the firm of Whitlock's, ironmongers, plumbers and so on, was to have a very large selection of Ford cars in their showroom. My great-grandfather was still running the taxi service in his eighties but was forced to retire after an article about him in the newspaper, with his photograph, had attracted the attention of 'the authorities', who felt that he was too old to continue any longer. In his retirement he lived with his wife in Penroses Villa, in Bodmin Street. One of his sons, John, had joined the business after a spell in Canada and, over the years, built it up into a full-scale garage with a fleet of buses which were still carrying country children to and from both schools in Holsworthy during my childhood.

My grandmother at this point was interrupted by the entry of the gardener, Mr. Box, a man in his seventies with white hair, bright eyes and glowing cheeks, wearing a collarless shirt and waistcoat and trousers from an old suit. It was winter and he had been clearing ice from the paths which he described as 'froozed'. They had a lively chat during which he responded to many of my grandmother's remarks with a slap of his thigh and an emphatic 'Eck-zackly!'

Suddenly the sound of Whitlock's siren in the market square alerted me to the time, the domestic help started to lay the table and the gardener declared, 'I'll be knocking,' and took his leave. The grocer's boy, who worked for my Aunt Clarice, arrived on an errand with fish and chips from the café and I returned home for my lunch.

Chapter 5

First Schools

'Are you sitting comfortably? Then I'll begin.' Many of us who were children in the fifties remember listening to the wireless as Daphne Oxenford or Dorothy Smith read the story after the *Berceuse* from Fauré's *Dolly Suite*, which introduced *Listen with Mother*. Whether it was this or other programmes such as *Housewife's Choice*, *Five to Ten* or *Woman's Hour* it was all very peaceful and well mannered, with an awareness by the broadcaster that he or she was a guest in your home.

The wireless stood on the mantelpiece over the stove in the kitchen, running off a large heavy battery which slid into an opening in the back like a drawer and Joyce, who still came each day to help with the housework, used to hum to it to such tunes as the 'Woody Woodpecker Song':

> Mmm mmm mmm mmm mmm [repeat],
> That's the Woody Woodpecker song . . .

It was part of an outlook on life that was very different from today and in which the wider world was less intrusive. The events of one's day mattered most, whatever was happening elsewhere. One of my first memories of Joyce, who lived on the Bude road close to where pylons had just been placed, is of riding with her on a swingboat at a small visiting fair, to which my father sometimes let a part of Upcott Field. I loved the swingboats' gentle swaying motion and their colourful pads for gripping, like the sally on a bell-ringer's rope. One year a little circus came to the field and, after sharing gooseberries with the manager's young son in our back garden earlier in the day, I watched spellbound as his older sister skipped on the back of a pony as it circled the arena; she also did some trick cycling.

I spent many hours playing with my toys on the kitchen floor, in the warmth of the stove. Sometimes my mother would be doing the ironing, pausing now and then to look through the window towards 'the top of North Road', as we called it, just before it took a right turn to skirt the churchyard, and watch familiar figures come or go – the headmaster of the primary school leaning forward and rubbing his hands; the Italian tailor, who had been a prisoner of war and stayed on and married a local girl, taking short quick steps with his head slightly bowed; and another man who would swing his arms across his chest as he walked.

After the morning's chores my mother would change into her smart going-out clothes and take me in a pushchair into the town, usually ending up at Elm Tree House for a cup of tea with my grandmother. Most of the people we met had time for a chat in the afternoon and I had to be patient as I was wheeled around the town. Most of the shops were owned by the shopkeeper whose sign appeared above the window or door, and all of these signs were different, as was the character of the shop within. One I particularly liked to go into was Saunder's shoe shop where the walls were stacked from floor to ceiling with boxes and where even more shoes were stored upstairs. As she went up the staircase Mrs. Walter, the lady in charge, would tell me in a whisper that she would have to go quietly as Father Christmas spent most of the year asleep up there. She had a very pretty assistant who, when I was a little older, would tighten my laces with nimble fingers and gaze up from her crouching position into my eyes as she asked whether I could move my toes.

Much of my time was spent playing alone since one of my sisters had made friends with girls at the primary school and the other one was already boarding at a convent school. During school holidays we met for 'lunch', at 11 o'clock, when we all had a biscuit or two together and drank Camp coffee or orange juice. We would try to persuade my mother to break away from her morning routine to join us but were not always successful since she was anxious to avoid 'getting behind'. Sometimes in the summer she would tear a rag in three and tie up in each piece a spoonful of Eiffel Tower lemonade power for us to suck as went off to play separately.

One day I was playing alone in the kitchen when I heard my mother talking to the rector's wife in the lounge, one of the two front rooms of the house. I gradually became aware that she was discussing my starting to attend the Rectory School. I resented being discussed by a complete stranger and had no desire to join the school. Was I not perfectly happy playing with my Dinky toys, marbles and other toys while a saucepan hissed and wheezed as the milk was slowly scalded? In case the rector's wife should come through to the kitchen I crawled under the table for the protection of the dark green chenille cloth which hung down over the sides.

Not surprisingly I had no choice in the matter and, at the start of the next term, I was led through the large, green, double gates into the yard of the rectory, which had recently been moved to a house at the end of Bodmin Street from the Manor Grounds opposite the church. So began my introduction to the larger world. On the second day I rebelled and kicked the gates shut each time an attempt was made to push or drag me through. I was taken home and, feeling ashamed, hid behind the coats and macintoshes hanging from the scullery door. My resistance was short-lived and by the end of the third day I was starting to feel part of the class.

There were about twelve of us, aged between three and five, and we were taught in a single classroom, housed in a separate building, by one teacher who was sometimes assisted by the rector's eldest daughter. We learnt to count with the aid of an abacus, to tell the time – I was worryingly slow at this – and to imitate 'a monkey climbing a stick or looking for nuts' (I'm still mystified by this!). Once a week we crossed the yard to the house, where the rector's wife read us stories. I remember one in particular called *The Three Sillies*. There was a mischievous boy called Rory, who, during an unsupervised period of break, set up a game of 'push-of-war' in which half of us pushed the classroom door from the outside and the rest pushed from within. The door came off its hinges and would have fallen on our heads but for the timely arrival of the rector.

Most of us went home for lunch and had to return for afternoon school at two o'clock. I kept a sharp eye on the kitchen clock and would grow anxious if my lunch was delayed – for instance, by a tradesman arriving at the back door. It was a long walk to the rectory since it was on the other side of the town. I had to make my way through the market square, past Elm Tree House and Penroses, by now Dr. Brown's house and surgery, and then down to the end of Bodmin Street, just before the second railway viaduct on the western side of the town. Through the kitchen window my mother would watch as I went up the road. If I met anybody I would stop them to ask the time. If this failed, I would call at a small shoe shop near the entrance to the square where there was a shopkeeper with a gold watch and chain who was happy to oblige. In spite of all this, I did arrive late one day. The rector, the Rev. Edward Royle, was already showing lantern slides in the darkened classroom. To my immense relief he accepted my apology with a smile. 'Films', as we called them, were frequently shown in the afternoon and we enjoyed them enormously. The only one I remember followed the narrative of *The Pilgrim's Progress* and a picture of a jolly fellow, whom we were told was an 'evangelist', standing at a sunny corner in a country lane, made a particular impression.

Our teacher had a son of about my own age with whom I became friendly. He lived at the end of a row of terraced cottages in Victoria Street, not far from the main square. We used to play with a rusty iron wheel just back from the pavement at the end of the street; it lay on its side and we took it in turns to sit on it for a ride as the other rotated it. The boy's father, a printer, whose shop occupied a site opposite the church, was one of the church vergers. Asked what he was going to be when he grew up my friend used to reply, 'A bishop.' The family moved

View of Bodmin Street. Penroses is the first house on the left

away and I lost touch with him, but I heard that he did attend a theological college.

Every Monday Mrs. Jennings, who was very jovial and would sometimes show my sisters how to skip, came to help with the weekly wash. Two zinc tubs were taken down from the wall and filled with hot, soapy water in the washroom, which, along with 'the office' (named after the purpose for which it had been built by Mr. Penhale), was detached from the main part of the house and stood across a little inner yard from the back door. When the washing had been soaked, stirred with a wooden pole, rinsed, wrung and placed on the washing line, my mother used, when I was very young, to put blue dye into the water of one of the tubs and I liked to float a wooden boat in it. Shirts, along with sheets, pillowcases and handkerchiefs, went off to the laundry and arrived back, pure white, in brown paper parcels. Later my mother had a boiler and did all of her washing at home, often using the little tub of Robin starch which lived on a shelf in the scullery.

The kitchen floor was concrete and every week it was swept and then polished with Cardinal polish. Occasionally the polish would be completely removed and the floor given a thorough cleaning with a scrubbing brush. Spring cleaning came round each year when, with two or three helpers, my mother gave the house a top-to-toe overhaul. Carpets were taken out on to the lawn and beaten thoroughly, mattresses were turned and pillows and bolsters were given a thorough shaking. Occasionally, the chimney sweep would arrive and I would go outside to watch for the brush to appear at the top of the chimney pot.

Regular visitors to the back door included the Corona man, with his familiar cry, various delivery boys and a jolly lantern-jawed man, delivering tyres which my father continued to buy from a friend he had made while based in Exeter. Coal and anthracite were delivered direct to the coal shed, which had a door opening on to the drive; and I would occasionally catch sight of the delivery man, blackened by the coal dust, wearing a sack over his head like a hood and carrying the sacks up the drive on his back. Once, when I was on my own in the house, a tramp called to ask politely and with a gentle smile for a glass of water which I supplied and he went off very contented.

On Market Day cattle were walked into the town and passed along North Road past Upcott on their way to the market. It was important for anyone living there to remember to shut the gates the night before. One day I looked out to see three or four cows charging about on the lawn outside the lounge window. I dashed eagerly out and, picking up a stick, ushered them back into the road.

I have already written about the time I used to spend in the yard. From here, during term time, I had heard the voices of the children in the playground of the primary school which was on the other side of the crossroads from where we lived. I was therefore quite excited when it was time for me to start attending. Since I had already attended the Rectory School I joined the second lowest class in the school and started to read about Dick and Dora in my *Happy Venture* reader. If boys misbehaved the teacher of this class, Miss Quance, ordered them to come to the front and 'punch the wall' as a punishment, which was really quite effective.

On my first day I took part in a game of football in the playground. This was played with a tennis ball and a new player joined the side which appeared to have the least number of players, first asking the captain's permission. As the ball rolled past by my foot I took aim and swept it into the corner of a goal chalked against the playground wall. 'Well done, bu-yee!' exclaimed a large country boy with red cheeks and greased hair. My heart swelled with pride! My eagerness to participate in playground games nearly got me into trouble, however. A few days later a crowd of boys stampeded across the yard diagonally; I followed them into the boys' lavatories only to discover that the headmaster had been pursuing them all around the playground after they had trespassed into the girls' section in the vicinity of their lavatories. They all received a beating which I escaped only through the intervention of Mrs. Jennings, who worked part-time at the school.

Winters were generally colder than they are today and I remember frequently grazing my frozen knuckles against the wall of the playground. On arriving in the morning, it was common for several boys to form a 'scram' to generate warmth; one or two of us would stand in a corner, facing inwards, and then the rest would pile in and push inwards. At the blow of a whistle we formed up in lines and, on instruction, filed into assembly, taken by the headmaster. After roll-call we sang a hymn such as *New Every Morning is the Love* or, my favourite, *Lead Me, Lord*, a Wesley setting of words from two of the psalms. The headmaster sometimes then exhorted the boys to make more effort, with reference to *Tired Tims* and *Weary Willies*, which I have since discovered were characters in a newspaper cartoon of former days.

There was more to life than school and, sometimes in different ways from the way they are today, children were made to feel important or special. In the afternoon of Carnival Day in November we competed in a fancy dress competition and a Fairy Queen presided. I won first prize as Captain Hook but did less well the following year as Regency Dandy, probably because a part of the costume consisted of the same coat and hat, though both had been much modified. A boy slightly older than me, who was watching the prize-giving, felt that an injustice had been committed and applauded me loudly as I collected second prize. In the evening, from an upstairs window at Elm Tree House, we looked down into Bodmin Street as the magical floats, lit by lamps or flames, passed below us in the darkness.

There were Sunday School outings – I still remember the bliss of a sunny afternoon spent paddling in the river at Yeolmbridge, followed by a walk up a steep hill for tea with jam and cream splits, and Christmas parties to which the girls wore dresses made from yards of net and where we played games like *The farmer's in his den*, or *Here we come gathering nuts in May*. Every Sunday most people attended either church or chapel in best clothes and on Palm Sunday we queued at the altar to receive a palm, which we took home with great pride.

Towards the back of the side lawn at Upcott stood a swing, constructed of a pair of tree trunks with peeling bark set into the ground and connected at the top by a wooden crossbar. On cloudless summer days I loved to swing high into the air and feel I was going out over the valley towards Windmill Hill. From this vantage point I could see, towards the end of the afternoon, the cows starting to wander in single file up the hill for milking. Through a window on the landing between my own and my sisters' bedroom I sometimes caught sight of steam rising in small puffs behind Windmill Hill, indicating that a train had left the station on its way to Okehampton and Exeter. The railway line, I knew, ran straight going away from me and the little puffs of cloud popped up gradually further and further along the ridge of the hill. It was as if the train was giving a parting signal that the world from which it had just passed was protected from interference from the world beyond.

Aston Clinton; The Mansion

Chapter 6

My Father's Village

I have already made reference to the fact that a part of my father really belonged to another age and his memories of his village childhood before the First World War. As we grew older he would sometimes talk to us about those days and relate to us anecdotes which, by repetition, became almost as real to us as our own memories.

Lady de Rothschild had been a widow for several years by the time my grandfather became an employee at the mansion. Her husband, Sir Anthony, was one of the sons of Nathan who had come to England from Frankfurt just before the end of the eighteenth century and, in perhaps one of the most extraordinary true life stories of all time, established within a few years the world's leading banking house. Sir Anthony had been financial adviser to the Prince of Wales and his two daughters were the prince's friends. Sir Anthony's nephew, Alfred, still entertained lavishly at neighbouring Halton Park.

Anthony and Louisa had bought the eighteenth-century house at Aston Clinton in 1853 and begun enlarging it by degrees. Among the guests they entertained were Benjamin Disraeli and his wife, who were frequent visitors, and the poet Matthew Arnold, son of the famous headmaster of Rugby School, whom Louisa would sometimes help to snap out of his periodical bouts of depression. Waddesdon Manor, which now belongs to the National Trust, was built some thirty years later by Ferdinand de Rothschild, the son of Anthony's cousin in Vienna.

My father's ancestors appear to have been living in or within a few miles of Aston Clinton for at least three hundred years but he knew nothing of this, family research being a more recent phenomenon. Among memorabilia in his desk he did keep a description of the village as it was towards the end of the nineteenth century, written in perfect handwriting by his Great-aunt Isabella. Starting from an arm of the canal at the southern end of the village she describes the wharf, the gas factory (for Sir Anthony's private use), the mansion – lately visited both by Prince Edward and his brother Alfred, the Duke of Edinburgh, the stables, the park surrounding the house skirted by a plantation and stretching to the churchyard, and the fourteenth-century church. From here she takes us on to the boys' school, a National School belonging to the rector of the parish, the girls' and infants' schools, supported by Lady de Rothschild, the Laundry and then the Soup Kitchen – 'where twenty girls from the school and ten boys each receive a good dinner for one penny.' Next come the post office, the Reading Room, where many lectures were given, and a row of cottages, built by Sir Anthony. This included the one in which my father was brought up.

The road on which my father lived was the main route connecting London with the centre of England, passing through Oxfordshire and eventually reaching Cheshire. It was not metalled and he remembered the first cars raising clouds of dust which got into the house and settled on the floor and furniture. In wet weather the surface of the road turned into mud, two or three inches deep. His family's cottage was one of three, the middle one being occupied by the Vince family. They bred little Japanese spaniels for Alfred de Rothschild who presented them to many ladies of his acquaintance, one of whom was Princess Alexandra.

The Rothschild staff and their families enjoyed a high standard of living for those days. Wages ranged upwards from about ten shillings a week, in most cases augmented by various perks such as coal. Staff working inside the mansion were comfortably accommodated there and cottages with large gardens, so that they could grow their own produce, were provided for those who were married. Bachelor gardeners slept in single rooms in the bothy, a long building in the grounds. Plants were made freely available and the head gardener, Mr. Warren, who had developed the art of growing strawberries in the greenhouse out of season, brought my father, when he was ill, a gift of runner beans in the middle of winter. At Christmas, children were asked what they would like as a present and they received such gifts as a train set, worth four or five pounds at that time, or bicycles. At Waddesdon, on the death of Baron Ferdinand in 1898, the head gardener received as much as five hundred pounds.

People in the village, however, particularly the younger ones, did not always show very much appreciation of the generosity of the Rothschilds. During the winter Alfred de Rothschild would offer any boy two pennies for every queen wasp he brought to his agent but many of them grumbled, 'I'm not doing anything for Alfred', perhaps missing the point that he was really doing something for them. My father knew where to find them, such as under the metal ivy which was attached to the front of a chalet on the estate, and collected them in matchboxes. He was so astounded to be given several shillings for his efforts that for several days he was afraid that someone would call and ask for the money back.

The children did not mind bowing or curtseying to the Rothschilds but resented being expected to show the same respect to anybody else. Miss Molique, daughter of a famous German violinist, had taught music to Lady de Rothschild's daughters and, when they had grown up, lived in a house called The Institution where she trained village girls for domestic service. She was often to be seen marching girls in a crocodile through the village.

'Where's your bow?' she asked a rough youth who, on passing them, had failed to touch his forelock.

'There's my bow,' he replied, flinging his cap on the ground and raising the dust in the process.

Village girls would sometimes hide behind the hedge to avoid having to curtsey. Being discreet had its advantages – one girl and her brother used to meet their mother, who worked for Miss Molique, at the back door of The Institution to receive two boiled eggs which they would eat in silence before creeping noiselessly away. In contrast to the people employed by the Rothschilds, families who depended on casual farm labour were exceptionally poor. My father remembered, in particular, one family recently arrived from London. The boys wore their father's cast-offs; the trousers were shortened unevenly at about knee level and a strand of cord fastened diagonally served as braces; the boots were so loose that, in order to prevent them from falling off, they had to pick their feet up almost vertically. Boys from poor families in the village were invited to take a clean pillowslip to the mansion on Saturday mornings to collect surplus food from the kitchen.

When we were all sitting around the kitchen table for a meal my father would sometimes dwell for a while on a memory then chuckle before telling us about a character or story from his village childhood.

Freddie Burnham was a hay and straw dealer. When he had been drinking heavily his friends had to pile him into his governess cart and his old mare would take him home without having to be driven. He had a servant called Tommy, who sat in the straw shed, even as late as midnight, to await his homecoming and to take the horse to the stable. My father, as he lay in bed in the dark, would sometimes hear a voice ring out in the clear country air calling 'Tommy!' every minute of so from several hundred yards up the road.

Bob Howe had a horse-drawn bus and used to take people from Aston Clinton to Aylesbury to catch the train. My father used to like to sit in the front with him. Once, as they went up the hill at Aylesbury, the bell kept ringing but Bob had determined not to stop to let any one off until they reached the top. When he pulled up they told him his wife had swung out over the tailboard into the road, halfway up the hill!

There were several merchants named Burnham, at least one of whom had coal delivered at Aylesbury Station in his own railway truck with his name painted on the side. One employed a haulier known as Geezer, who used to drive a horse and butt loaded with hay and straw to the mews of one of the London residences of the Rothschilds and return with horse manure for their gardens and pastures. After a day's work he was always willing to allow my father and his friends to take his horses to the fields, about half a mile away. My father recalled once trying to restrain one of the horses attached to a wagon while Geezer tried to put back a huge lump of coal which had fallen off the back. Every time he came near, the old horse trotted a few steps ahead, my father not having the strength to hold it. To make matters worse Geezer started to laugh. So there they were, my father clutching the reins with both hands and Geezer bent double with the weight of the coal, struggling along the road behind the cart and shouting between spasms of laughter, 'Hold the horse! Hold the horse!'

There was also a grocer named Goodson, who appeared in the local carnival with a friend – both wore long beards and animal skins and rode wooden bicycles – and whose name was carved in letters an inch deep on the side of his wooden van. He was known as Old Ingie, having been christened Old England as were some of his ancestors, going back at least to the eighteenth century. He was skilful with his hands and used to make tin soldiers. When batting at a village cricket match he grunted each time he played the ball and in fun boys on the boundary used to grunt in a chorus at the same time.

Like me, my father had two elder sisters. His great-grandfather, on his mother's side, also lived in the cottage. He was a living link with a past which stretched back almost to the Napoleonic Wars, having been born in 1821 and dying at the age of ninety-three, three and a half months before the outbreak of the First World War. In his old age he could still dig an allotment and bring home a sack of potatoes on his back. When once asked if he were not tired of life he replied simply, 'My life is as sweet to me as yours is to you'. One of his daughters, my father's maternal grandmother, was a straw plaiter, a very hard way to earn a living. She died in her forties before my father was born. One of her daughters, my grandmother's sister Alice, married a baker and my father loved riding around the Chilterns on top of his uncle's horse-drawn van, warmed by the bread beneath and enjoying its delicious smell. This uncle gave up the bakery and became landlord of the Station Hotel at Princes Risborough. He was also captain of the local fire brigade. Late in life he had a lady friend in London whom he regularly visited. Each time he left for the railway station, just across the road from the hotel, in his best suit and carrying a bunch of flowers, his wife and daughter could be seen in a front window pointing after him and clutching their sides with laughter.

The use of straw to make boaters and other hats, centred on Luton and Dunstable, had provided a lot of employment before the arrival of the Rothschilds and there were many plaiters, including very young children, and dealers in the area. If a child asked to go out to play the reply would be, 'Not until you've done your plait.'

Once a year the church in Aston Clinton organised a Sunday school outing to Aldbury Common, about six miles away. Two haycarts were washed out and polished and the children, twenty in each cart, sat on fresh straw, three or four in a row. Each cart was drawn by a shire horse, which walked mostly but, at the flick of the reins, would break into a trot. At Aldbury the children competed in various sports for a set of fishing rods or a walking stick. My father always won the hundred yards. After tea they scrambled for sweets. He sometimes talked about the walks he used to take around Aston Clinton and, when on holiday, the farm of one of his mother's cousins at Hartwell. On one of these, where a bridleway passed into a field, the countryside seemed to stretch away right into the heart of England. Looking back, towards the end of his life, my father wrote the following poem:

Upon a golden summer day,
The air was sweet with new-mown hay
And hedgerows in their summer dress
Danced to the gentle winds' caress;
The happy lark sang in the sky
While peewits made their plaintive cry.

I'd left the village far behind,
Wishing solitude to find,
The bridleway led to the plain
Where horses rested free from strain,
Here peace took me by the hand
And showed me life as Nature planned.

I saw the steeple far away,
'twas built in Harry Tudor's day,
While oak and ash within the glade
Gave the cattle welcome shade,
In this haven few men trod
It was a place to walk with God.

The pre-war idyll, or, as my father often said, the bad old days of poverty for many, was about to end with the approach of the war. Lord Rothschild, who lived at Tring Park, and Alfred de Rothschild donated large areas of parkland for military training for the duration of the war and Aston Clinton became a divisional headquarters. Anthony Hall, built by Lady de Rothschild in the eighteen-eighties, became a centre for the YMCA where hundreds of soldiers received their last hot meals under the management of my grandmother and her band of helpers. The YMCA was a great source of comfort to the young soldiers about to go 'out there'. A lady living in Aston Clinton over sixty years later still recalled vividly the sight of one of my aunts trying to console a young man who was sobbing his heart out because he had to go to the front the next day.

ANTHONY HALL. ASTON CLINTON.

Photo Collier.

Anthony Hall in the early 1900s

My father recalled with sadness the fate of a few of the young men he had come to know well and who had lost their lives in the war – his cousin Alf from Princes Risborough, who had stood by a chest-high pile of books which he had won at school to have his photograph taken by the local newspaper; Alf Burnham, who simply disappeared with his horse, before the eyes of his second cousin Len, in Gallipoli when a shell exploded; Micky Bandy, who with his brother Percy won all the prizes for sports – Micky had once done my father the 'honour' of leaping over him while he was walking down the road and turned and given him a grin; there was also a local teacher and goalkeeper for the local team, who, to the tune of *Clementine*, had sung to the daughter of the village policeman:

> Oh, my Lily, Oh, my Lily,
> Do not be the least afraid,
> Just remember, just remember
> That you are a p'liceman's maid!

She took him to court for this, where he was fined. He received a commission and became one of the thousands of lieutenants who were mown down as they led their troops over the top.

Like many others my father lied about his age and volunteered for army service but was not at first accepted. In 1918 he tried again and, after training on Salisbury Plain, was sent to the Rhine Army Border Guard at Cologne. He was too late to see action and in 1919 returned to his job at an auctioneer's office in Tring, where he became much in demand as secretary to the football club, cricket club and others.

After the war Lady de Rothschild's daughters were spending only a few weeks a year at Aston Clinton and so decided to sell. The mansion became first a private school and eventually, after being used for various other purposes, was deliberately razed to the ground as nobody was either able or willing to afford its upkeep. Alfred de Rothschild had died in 1918 and had left the Halton estate to his nephew Lionel. He had never liked the property and was keen to sell it quickly. It was, however, in a dreadful condition after army occupation and the government, therefore, was able to acquire it at a ridiculously low price to use as a Royal Air Force training centre.

Chapter 7

We Release a Field and Gain a Beach

One Saturday morning after breakfast, my father, who was still selling oil, announced that he had bought a beach. 'Where is it?', 'Is it sandy?', 'Will we be able to bathe there?' were the inevitable questions.

At the top of Belle Vue in Bude, on the corner with Princes Street, was a large shop known as The Emporium (now The Merchantman) unusually for those days selling a variety of goods. It was owned by friends of my parents whom we knew as Auntie Nellie (actually a distant relative) and Uncle Frank. A sand and gravel business just south of Widemouth had come up for sale and these friends were willing to make my father a loan to enable him to buy it on one condition – in the words of Auntie Nellie to her husband, 'You aren't to charge any interest, Frank!'

The assets of the business comprised the beach rights, the cliffs and adjoining fields, an office, a stone-crusher, five lorries and a few sledgehammers and shovels. The beach itself was shingle although it was possible, at low tide, at a time when it was too dangerous for us to bathe, to clamber over slippery rocks to reach a thin strip of sand at the edge of the sea. Two hardy ladies used to ask, in the early days, for my father's permission to swim in a narrow and deep natural pool which they had discovered in the rocks and which they called The Lagoon, but we were content to leave it to the crabs and lobsters.

A stream ran down the valley to the beach, opening out into a large pond where on one occasion I saw a trout rise. I liked to bounce flat stones across the surface or throw large ones as far as I could into the centre to watch the concentric rings ripple towards the edge. Running my fingers through the thick, long grass in the bank rising steeply on one side of the stream I would find sea purses which had blown out of the sea and buried themselves there. Primroses covered the banks of the stream in spring and further up, where the valley was thickly wooded, were bluebells. The area between the stream and my father's office was filled with blackberry and sloe bushes and away from the edge of the cliff lay impenetrable gorse, a haven for such birds as linnets and stonechats. Behind the office, with a view across the beach to the rocks, where oystercatchers piped and strutted throughout the day, was a sheltered grassy area for sunbathing, christened, by my younger sister, Dingley Dell, after the house in *The Pickwick Papers*. Apart from gravel, the sea washed up numerous glass balls, green or white, sometimes still connected to a piece of fishing net, and we spread them about the garden at Upcott, hung them up in the open garage which by now had replaced the hay shed, or stored them in boxes to give to anyone who wanted them. My father also brought home some little nuggets of 'gold' – copper-iron sulphide or fool's gold – and at first I thought I was going to be very rich. More profitable were cuttlefish, which I scrubbed until they were pure white and packed into boxes for sending off to a pet shop in Reading.

My father had by now released Upcott Field to the football club, which at the beginning of the war had lost its playing field when land was requisitioned to accommodate a unit of the Somerset Yeomanry. Henceforth, spectators poured down the road from the direction of the town and cars were parked outside our house every Saturday afternoon. As I have said, I was able to watch matches through the fence in the back garden which had spread out to incorporate the former chicken run. If the ball came over, the game was suspended as I retrieved it from the cabbages and kicked it back. If I miskicked it into the fence, I would ignore the cries of 'Throw it! Throw it!' and carry on kicking a second or even third time until I cleared it. My father was sometimes amazed by the violent shouts of some of the men in the crowd at football matches, 'Windy!' or 'Where's your specs, ref!' were two of the milder forms of criticism. He once asked one of our local doctors, a Dr. Craddock, who was somewhat revered for his wisdom, why he thought they did it. 'Somebody's been shouting at them all week,' he said, 'now it's their turn.'

It was not widely known at the time that Dr. Craddock had, as a young doctor, assisted Dr. Alexander Fleming with his experiments leading to the discovery of penicillin. The two became friends and Sir Alexander used subsequently to visit him at his home, Bodmeyrick, in North Road.

In the summer of 1951 my father decided to take us to see the Festival of Britain. On the night before our departure he warned us that we would have an early start. We set off in semi-darkness and swept quietly along the empty roads towards Exeter, looking out for the odd buzzard, perched on top of a telegraph pole. As we continued, others cars gradually began to appear on the road. These were the days when one might be stuck for miles on the A30 in a queue of cars which had built up behind a lorry or a pair of slow-moving Austin Sevens. Foolish drivers would try to work their way up the queue, forcing their way back in between two cars if something came in the opposite direction. There was little advantage to be gained in this and I remember catching up with one such car again after several miles, by this time only a few cars ahead, as we came to drive through Salisbury. Only as we came nearer to London did single traffic give way to dual carriageways. We arrived at the Cumberland Hotel, in those days a place of extreme luxury with a family atmosphere, at about four in the afternoon. We had settled into our rooms – I shared one with my sisters – when there was a knock at the door and a television was delivered. This was the first time that we had seen one; we turned the knob and watched with fascination as blurred white figures appeared and moved about in a grey fog. A little later my father came in and said, 'Oh, *you've* got it!' He had requested it in order to watch the test match and it had been delivered to the wrong room.

I remember more of the funfair at the Festival Gardens in Battersea Park than the actual festival although I do recall drinking fresh milk, much to our surprise, from a herd of cows from Carey Barton, a farm only a few miles from Holsworthy on the road to Launceston. One evening we queued outside the Drury Lane Theatre for tickets – returns or perhaps a stool in the slips – to see *Carousel* and were entertained by buskers.

I had never experienced London buses, with the conductors calling out all the stops, helping people on and off and engaging in friendly chat with passengers – 'salt of the earth', my father called them. Then there were the tube trains and the escalators at the tube stations and in the department stores and the revolving doors; it was all very exciting. At the hotel I started riding up and down continuously in one of the lifts. The lift man eventually ran out of patience and, after waiting for it to empty, gave me a good ticking off. His attitude changed abruptly when a gentleman and lady, stepping in at the next stop, found me in tears. The visit to London gave me further experience of meeting Americans and I was delighted by their uncomplicated approach to life, asking right out, 'Which part are you folks from?' In contrast, my mother had been doing her best to disguise her Devonshire accent, for these were the days when the benchmark for standard speech was the Queen's English, and she was taken aback when somebody in the hotel foyer asked her from which part of Devon she had come!

London had yet to become swamped by too many visitors and Londoners, each living in their own distinct community, not unlike the country village, still had a common sense of identity. Quick-witted by nature and rightly proud after their resilience during the Blitz and other wartime experiences, they were more appreciated in those days for what they were, and were, therefore, still able to be friendly and welcoming to outsiders.

Like most young people in Holsworthy, one event I looked forward to every year was the fair. I especially liked the Noah's Ark and the Dodgems, with its distinctive smell and blaring music, and the Hall of Mirrors. I never won anything at the stalls but, in order to be sure of bringing something home, paid for a choice at the Pick-a-Cork or Lucky Dip. There was always a boxing booth, but, after the boy who had applauded me at the Carnival had been seen coming out from a bout shaking his head at the massacre he had just witnessed, it was some time before I ventured in to watch. One year I went up to look around the fair on the night before its opening and was lurking around one stall which a man was still erecting when he asked me to help him by just getting hold of the end of a beam. Once this had been attached he asked me to do two or three more things, saying each time that this would be the last, until I found myself enclosed within the perimeter of the stall. His manner then changed completely and he started to give me curt instructions, complaining if I did not follow them to the letter. I started to feel a growing sense of panic. Thinking I could not escape, he went off, saying he would be back shortly. After he had gone, I managed, with an effort, to climb over the side of the stall and, after running all the way home, spent some time relaxing on the swing with a great sense of relief.

I became a frequent visitor to the shops in Holsworthy, often on errands for my mother. Mr. Vivian, at his grocery store, always had time for a chat about sport and one of his assistants, Frank Rowland, who played in the town band, used to promise in his slightly shy manner to give me his old cornet. At Tickner's toy shop I called, in vain, for several months to see if the octopus had arrived to complete my diver-and-octopus set; this consisted of a diver which went up or down in the water in a bottle by putting in or pulling out the cork while the octopus did the opposite. Mr. and Mrs. Tickner liked talking to children and I sometimes wondered if that was why they ran the shop as it was never very busy. I remember his telling me about the Robin Hood Gate of Richmond Park, named after the nearby Robin Hood Inn. I had seen the Disney film of *Robin Hood* at the cinema in Bodmin Street, but had no idea at the time that the actor, Richard

The Square on Market Day

Todd, who played the hero had, as a boy, once lived in the house I knew of as Dr. Evans's, opposite the entrance to the Manor Grounds.

When my football was flat I slid back the doors, on their well-oiled grooves, of Oliver's, the saddler and tobacconist, where father and son, one echoing the other, politely addressed me in their gentle Devonshire drawl as 'Maaster Axtell'. When I picked the ball up a couple of days later it bounced perfectly and was thoroughly renovated, with a new lace and treated with dubbin. I had my hair cut at the barber's, a section of the business premises still referred to by locals today as Hill's Papershop, for threepence; the men were charged a shilling. Sometimes they would have a word with the barber and then ask, 'Are you in a hurry, boy?' I learned from experience to answer 'Yes!' Another saddler and tobacconist, in Fore Street, was Tom Rowland who, in his old age, used to help my father with the digging in the back garden. When I was learning to dig I used to wear myself out within about half an hour and my father told me that this quiet old gentleman would work very slowly and patiently but that by the end of the day he would have covered a large area. Sometimes I would go to the library, a little room tucked in off the road just beyond a raised walkway in Chapel Street. It had once been the Wesleyan Day School. Along with the distinctive smell of library books there was a friendly atmosphere, as there is today in the library which for the last thirty years has stood opposite the church. Books were divided into *Fiction* and *Non-Fiction*. I was always drawn to the former which, representing feelings and imagination, seemed more real to me than *Non-Fiction*, which merely contained well-arranged facts.

Both of my sisters were now attending convent school and two or three times a term my parents and I would travel by car to Bideford to see them. When very young, I used to wonder how my father could travel so far without losing his way. A gravel drive through the grounds, with shrubs and trees on either side, led to the 'Commons' which housed the junior girls and, on Saturday afternoons, they would crowd the windows, watching out for cars arriving to take girls out for the afternoon. Once, a tall nun whose voluminous black habit frightened me a little, took my hand and led me into the house and along a winding corridor, past open doorways packed with girls, to the kitchen. Here she went to the drawer of a scrubbed wooden table, took out something and gave it to me. 'A blood orange!' she said kindly, and I, in my childish ignorance, recoiled in horror! The return journey, as the skies grew dark, seemed a long one. My parents were silent. From the back seat I watched the cats' eyes grow brighter as the light faded and, as we passed through Holsworthy Beacon, the silhouette of Holsworthy Church tower came into view. In the western sky the first star glowed, bigger and brighter than those which would follow. For me it represented the Star of Bethlehem.

Christmas was a time when my grandparents drew their children and their families from various parts of the country under one roof at Elm Tree House. It was the only time of year when all the bedrooms were fully occupied, the younger daughters returning to the rooms they had had as teenagers and the rest of us fitting in as best we could.

I had about twenty cousins and we were divided into two categories. First there were the under-fives who believed in the Santa who came after lunch to give out the Christmas presents from around the Christmas tree in the large bay window in the lounge on the first floor, and left to a chorus of *For he's a jolly good fellow*! This role was played by Ben Oke, who was a printer and was also well used to entertaining in costume; subsequently, a younger man who was related by marriage to my Aunt Barbara took over. The older cousins, over five years of age, were those who believed only in the true Santa who came when we were asleep at night to fill our stockings, and then disappeared as quietly as he had come. One Christmas I had decided to try to stay awake until he came. As I listened to water trickling through a pipe I imagined several times that I heard the distant jingle of sleigh bells. The grandfather clock along the corridor struck several times. I fell asleep. When I awoke it was very dark and a rustling sound at my feet indicated the presence of somebody in the room. Scarcely daring to breathe, I turned my head and with one eye discerned a stooping figure in a dark red coat filling my stocking. He seemed to be redolent of sweat and leather and totally absorbed in fulfilling his great toil. I closed my eyes and savoured the thought. I had seen the real Father Christmas!

At lunchtime on Christmas Day we went to the kitchen at the sound of the gong to collect our Christmas dinner. We carried the full plates along the back passage and down three steps with brass strips along the front of them, into the dining room to sit at a table which was large enough to accommodate the entire family. After the Christmas pudding we lit indoor fireworks and listened to one of my uncles, who had been in the merchant navy, as he told us a tale, pausing occasionally to puff on a cigar. He was good at this and I remember one about a ghost which appeared when he was keeping solitary watch at night, halfway across the Atlantic Ocean. In the evening, one of my sisters presented a Nativity play, into which we had been dragooned and for which we were rigorously drilled by her over the preceding days. When I was a little older I amused my female cousins with a conjuring display which contained as many errors as those orchestrated in a performance by Tommy Cooper! On Boxing Day I liked to sit in the bay window of the lounge, now emptied of presents, and look down on the street below to where the hounds and huntsmen would shortly pass at the head of the traditional meet.

Winter evenings with my parents were spent in front of a log fire playing rummy, draughts or halma. Sometimes we flung on a piece of driftwood, brought back from the beach, and might see a green or blue flame or hear a sudden hiss or a loud report as a spark leapt out and burnt another black mark on the carpet. We needed no other entertainment although, in some moods, as the wind whistled around the house and found its way through the cracks under the doors, talk might turn rather depressingly to deaths or illnesses. 'Gone to Plymouth', when talking of a relative or somebody we all knew in the town, was a phrase often used, meaning gone to the hospital for an operation. At night, when both my sisters were away at school, I was alone upstairs and my room seemed very dark as I listened to the tall cypress trees in the drive just outside my window and waited patiently for the distant hum of a car approaching from either direction. When at last one did drive past, its lights would form the shadow of the window frame on the wall and then move it swiftly across the walls and ceiling, providing temporary relief from the darkness.

I believe that we were among the first of those in Holsworthy to have television. It is difficult to convey to those who now take it for granted the sense of excitement which we felt waiting for the test card to appear in the afternoon. As it had been with the wireless, the people who appeared on our television screens did so as guests in our homes and this was reflected in their manners. Children's programmes were presented by the gentle-eyed and beautifully spoken Jennifer Gay who won my heart, as she did those of many of the nation's boys and youths at the time. After school I used to invite a friend and his slightly older sister to come home with me to watch favourite Westerns. Sadly their father, a ventriloquist who performed in front of us all at a birthday party for one of them, died of cancer and the family moved away. On Saturdays, *Whirligig* alternated with *Saturday Special* while on Sundays, as we enjoyed a weekly treat in the winter, dipping sticks of celery into a little salt, we watched *Muffin the Mule*. The nearest we got to soap operas was *The Appleyards* and later *The Grove Family*. Rescheduling was almost unheard of and I remember being taken completely by surprise when the coverage of the historic test match, at which Jim Laker took all ten Australian wickets in the second innings, after taking nine in the first, was interrupted so that Andy Pandy could make his afternoon appearance at the usual time.

We had had a television for a year by the time of the Coronation and watched it throughout the day. My father had planted red, white and blue sweet peas in the front garden to mark the occasion. Extra chairs were brought through to the lounge to seat some friends of my parents, Mr. and Mrs. Petherbridge, who had been invited to watch the event with us. We sat there throughout the best part of the day, mostly silent as if we were actually in Westminster Abbey, and we were moved by the young queen's beauty and humility. My mother brought in tea, orange squash and sandwiches. Afterwards we went down Sanders Lane to the grounds of the Senior School where I participated in a pillow fight on a greasy pole and watched the three-legged races. After rain earlier the sun had suddenly come out. It was like a bright omen for the future.

Looking north from the church tower; 'Upcott' and 'Upcott Field' in the middle distance

Chapter 8

Boys in a Country Town

Life is never perfect and even those of us who cling to memories of our childhood know that there were many fairly minor things which we would not like to have to put up with again. But after another world war had come close to destroying the world as we know it, and would have done so but for the courage and self-sacrifice of those who fought for it, this time of peace was very special.

There was a desire to live a day at a time and, without shutting out the major events in the world at large which these days are thrust upon us relentlessly, not to allow them to dominate our lives.

This is not to say that we were indifferent to major events like the Lynton and Lynmouth flood disaster in the summer of 1952, when more than thirty people lost their lives and many more were made homeless. In the same year, just weeks before Christmas, we were horrified by pictures of people in London struggling to go about their daily business, handkerchiefs over their noses and mouths, in what was known as the Great Smog. This claimed an estimated four thousand lives.

The happiest days of my childhood occurred during summer holidays when we spent between two and four weeks at our old caravan on the coast at Widemouth. How it had come to be there I do not know but we started to have our holidays there when I was very young after my parents had sold a wooden holiday bungalow across the road from the caravan – the work involved in cleaning it and tidying up the garden had been too much. To reach Widemouth we turned off the Bude road at Red Post and headed towards Launceston, crossing over the railway line and the path of the former Bude Canal, before turning right and following the quiet lanes for the rest of the way.

The caravan and the three wooden huts, which housed the kitchen, an extra bedroom and at a little distance away the lavatory, were all tucked under a hedge and surrounded by a fence to keep out the cows. The wheels of the caravan were supported by wooden stilts and a short flight of steps led up to the doorway; its travelling days were over. Inside it was divided into three by partitions of dark-stained wood, which gave off an acrid smell in hot weather – a central area with a washbasin and room for a table, and two bedrooms. At each end a little window opened upwards on stiff hinges just above the level of the bed. It was not the prettiest caravan you ever saw but that only made it seem all the more real. I used to sit on one of the shafts at the front and imagine taking it along the country lanes along which it had once travelled. I shared one of the bedrooms with my younger sister. In the mornings we would sometimes wake to the sound of grass being torn and look out of the window to find that the cows had broken through the fence and were grazing under our very noses. The hedge near the gate to the field had broken down over the years and on top were rusty, iron fences twisted and bent by the movement of the soil and the weight of the cows which had rubbed against them. Over this a kestrel sometimes hovered.

Looking out from the caravan to the right there was a view of the coast road, rising steeply in a series of double bends on its way to Crackington Haven, and the green cliffs to the west of Millook. On the other side of the road a tractor might be seen crawling silently up and down a field, the shape of which had become engraved on my subconscious. I used to watch out for the arrival on a distant hill of the tents of a Scouts group. To me this was an Indian camp and I would imagine small clouds to be smoke signals.

We did not always go to the beach in the morning. My sister and I would sometimes explore the hedgerows in the field then wander further down the field through the thistles and look back at the caravan slowly disappearing from sight, forgetting the time of day, until we reached the stream at the bottom where the cows were standing to keep cool. Later we would hear the sound of my mother's voice floating over the brow of the hill and calling us to lunch. If we did go to the beach for a morning bathe we went down a steep path through gorse and brambles and over a stile. Beyond this the path soon yielded to sand and opened out in front of Black Rock to take us on to a beach which was usually deserted at that time of day. How short the walk seemed on the way down, and how long at the end of the morning, when we dragged our tired limbs back up again, our mouths tingling with salt and longing for the taste of fresh water. In the afternoon we usually went by car to the furthest beach, which we called Third Beach, and drove down a path to park behind a small row of dark green wooden huts which are still there over fifty years later. There we took up our favourite position under the cliff near the old Salthouse.

The fish and chip van came round twice a week and I used to swing on the gate to the field, listening for the sound of the handbell rung by the driver. We did not mind if it rained. During the day we played cards in the caravan and my father might appear in the afternoon with a dozen small bars of chocolate. In the evening he might take us to the Picture House in Bude and, on returning in the dark, we would go to bed, later than usual, and lie awake listening to the rain beating on the caravan roof. If my father was away for the day working we sometimes caught the bus to Bude. Standing at the bus stop at the corner where the main road turns away from the coast, we would wait for it to appear on the skyline, hoping it would be a double-decker. Meanwhile we threw burrs at each other to pass the time. Lundy Island was usually visible and we would look across for a weather forecast:

> Lundy high, sign of dry;
> Lundy low, sign of snow;
> Lundy plain, sign of rain;
> Lundy haze, fine for days.

These were carefree days and, except for one year when I became fatigued by the heat, we were always sorry to leave. When we did return Upcott seemed very strange; the rooms were larger than we had remembered them and we seemed to hear a slight echo to our voices.

The teacher with whom I spent most of my primary school years was a kindly spinster, wiry and full of nervous energy. Her face was lined with care but, on occasions, her eyes would shine lovingly through her anxiety from behind her gold-rimmed spectacles. Her inability to frighten us led her to resort to occasional smacks behind our knees with a ruler which merely stung a little. Her ultimate deterrent was to send us out of the room into the corridor from where the next step could be the headmaster's study and a beating. On being sent out one day for laughing at an inappropriate moment, I was standing anxiously outside the door with my ears alert when I heard the sound of his approaching footsteps. I began to walk slowly down the corridor towards the door leading to the playground, as if I were on the way to the lavatories. When the danger had passed I tiptoed back again and had just arrived at the classroom door when it opened, the worried face of Miss Piper appeared, and she beckoned me quickly inside again. It was to this teacher that I owed mastery of most of my tables and she gave me one of those first boosts of confidence which remain with us for the rest of our lives when, on first hearing me read a story, she declared that I was doing so well that I should skip a whole book. Each day after lunch we had to rest, which involved leaning forward on one's desk and placing one's head on one's arms. This posture was also adopted by a child who was feeling sick or had a headache. One girl spent the entire morning burying her face in her arms after the news of the death of King George VI. When asked by Miss Piper what the matter was she said simply, 'I'm sad, miss.'

I was at that time as typical a small country town boy as you might find, with an impish grin and tousled hair. I wore a bottle green corduroy jerkin with a zip down the front and two breast pockets, and I covered it with badges – Shell, Esso, I-Spy and numerous others, as well as metal bottle tops, bright red and green, attached by removing the cork disk and pressing it back in again from the inside of the garment. One week I was awarded a school badge labelled 'Courtesy', but had to forfeit it after two days for committing an indiscretion, not surprisingly since I did not know what the word 'courtesy' meant.

Rationing was gradually phased out in the early fifties, but we still did not have many treats. Sweets continued to be rationed until 1953. I became very popular during July when on a few occasions I would arrive in the playground with a bag of gooseberries which I had picked from the back garden. Within a few seconds I would be surrounded by a crowd of anxious boys, with outstretched hands, shouting out my name and repeating, 'You know *me*!' Each day after school, if it was not raining, I went off to the park or in autumn, perhaps, across the road to the horse chestnut to try to knock down some conkers with a stick. Boys have always stolen apples and the orchard at the end of our garden bordered on to the park and so was especially vulnerable. A gang of boys used to assemble on the other side of our hedge and persuade one of the smaller ones to push his way through a drainage hole into our orchard to collect them. They continued to help themselves occasionally although my father used to try to stop it by throwing windfalls over the hedge on to the grass in the park.

At around this time I had begun to have nightmares, waking up in a sweat and calling out loudly. They began after I had seen the film *Kim*, based on the book by Kipling, at the cinema. I believe it was either Dr. Brown or a Dr. Pearson who suggested to my parents that I went up to Elm Tree House to sleep. Here, at the end of the upstairs corridor, although a long way from where my grandparents were seated in the breakfast room, I went off to sleep perfectly happily. One of the upstairs rooms at Elm Tree House was hired out to a dentist who came up twice a week from Bude. It was strange to see people, some of them complete strangers, coming and going to the waiting room which was the lounge in which we spent so much time at Christmas. When I waited there alone for treatment, sometimes for an hour or more, it felt very big and empty. I had two teeth out by gas on one occasion and nearly choked to death while I was still unconscious. I knew nothing about it until I awoke some time later to find myself in a nearby bedroom feeling very sick. When I was talking to my grandmother about it she told me about the time when she had had her first tooth 'pulled' as a girl by Dr. Owen Kingdon. There was no gas then and his wife took her into the front room of the house saying, 'You mustn't make a sound or you will wake up the baby.'

During school holidays one or other of a pair of brothers, who also lived in North Road, slightly nearer the town, would sometimes call at the back door and ask me to come out to play. One was slightly older than me and the other slightly younger. Two of us would frequently fall out with the third and I would not see them for a while. Then they would grow bored with each other's company and one of them would reappear at the back door to make it up. We spent much of our time in the cellar of their old home at the top of North Road, which could be entered from the outside by a short flight of slate steps and smelt of mould. Here we painted a wooden sword silver, made bows and arrows from young willow branches cut from the hedgerow, carved whistles, repaired our bicycles or just discussed what we *would* do.

One day I walked ahead of my companions as we went down a path which starts alongside the churchyard and runs down to the stream at Church Bridges, where a weir breaks the flow of the water and creates a wide pool. As I arrived quietly and alone, my eyes rested for a few moments upon a beautiful gold and blue bird perched quite still over the middle of the pool. It was obviously a kingfisher but, as I looked at it, it appeared to be a large bird in my mind's eye. It is the only experience I have had of what I believe the poet William Blake meant by 'two-fold vision'.

It was a fine day and we had decided to be cowboys, re-enacting the Westerns we had watched at the cinema. At the farm across the road, which belonged to Mr. Edwin Kivell, we staged a gun battle in the farmyard then wandered down across the fields, crossed the stream at a point where we had built stepping stones, and made our way up the side of Windmill Hill. Along the edge of this field ran a ditch and we filled our cowboy hats for a drink with the water tumbling over a stone, fortunately not suffering any ill effects. 'White water', according to the dubious lore we had learned from Westerns, was safe to drink. As we crossed another field we heard the sound of voices across the valley – 'Indians' – and decided to stalk them under the cover of the hedge. We followed them at a safe distance until they reached the road of Waterloo Hill where they struck off in the direction of their homes on the far side of the football field. We crossed the road to the entrance to the local dump. A notice on the gate read, 'Private Property, Trespassers Will Be Prosecuted'. A sense of the forbidden and the possibility of being found out added an extra element of excitement. We climbed over and walked along a drive bordered by rhododendrons and grassy mounds – the remnants of the recreation area known as Kingswood Meadow. The small lake, on which there had once been a boat and where swans had nested, was now filled with refuse. We skidded down the side of a small mountain of rubble and re-climbed it several times to repeat the exercise until we heard the sound of a motor getting louder as it came nearer – the dust wagon. As pre-arranged, we scuttled off into the rhododendrons to 'spy'. We emerged when the coast was clear and had just returned to the road when three of the boys whom we thought had all gone back to their homes (the 'Indians') charged up to us with their fists flying and I found myself fending off a small boy with a shiny brown face and greased hair as he pummelled my ribcage. My friends fought off their attackers who decided to run for it.

The houses in which the boys who had attacked us lived, on the other side of the football field, had been converted after the war from the prisoner of war huts, with their concrete walls, into comfortable homes, each with a separate garden. Some had been subdivided and provided accommodation for two families. By about the mid-fifties people were starting to move on to the fresh housing which was being built to the west of the town – Glebelands, built on fields formerly known as Pa'sons Hams, and Pins Park. As the converted huts were knocked down they were replaced by new houses, nearby or on the same site, such as Stanhope Close. The process took quite some time; it was nearly ten years before the last people moved out of the original homes. A few of the huts came to be used for other purposes – a hospital clothing factory, formed by joining together half a dozen of them, and a grocer's shop; Whitlock's Dairy in neighbouring Dobles Lane, carried on using one for storage. The firm of A.W. Bent, now in Stratton, set up the clothing factory in the mid-sixties after relocating from Luton. It employed a large number of women, some from the town; others came in by train, while the service was still running; later, three vans used to collect them from Bradworthy and Bude.

But these developments were only just beginning to happen at the time when we were wandering around the fields close to the town. We spent many hours in the wood on the far side of the field behind the farm, crossing the field at the top and climbing over a hedge. In spring, the floor of the wood was covered with bluebells. It was on a steep slope which ended abruptly above a disused quarry. On a cold day in winter we found, hanging from the ceiling of a cave in an outcrop of rock, jagged icicles which we broke off and used as swords. We knew the best parts of the rivers for fishing with jam jars for 'tom thumbs', minnows and sticklebacks, and the ponds where we would be able to find newts with yellow undersides, water skaters, water scorpions, water boatmen and whirligig beetles. Wherever there was water, dragonflies hovered.

My friends' uncle played in the local bowls team and told them that somebody had been breaking into the hut on the bowling green which stood at the far end of the park. We decided to catch the intruders red-handed. The floor of the hut was covered with fine, dry earth and we scraped this up and made paper 'grenades' with which to attack the intruders. Perhaps they got wind of us for, after several evenings of lying in wait without success, we gave up. After our recent encounter at Waterloo Hill some boys had decided to challenge us to a 'friendly' boxing match in one of the remaining prisoner of war huts which stood empty. We arrived early and left our bicycles out of sight behind the hedge. After the first bout it was my turn but the boy who stepped forward was a lot bigger than me. The older of my two friends said that they must find someone more suitable while we practised sparring.

After a few mock blows he leant across to me and whispered, 'When I say so, scram!' He motioned to his brother, who started to move slowly towards the door. 'Now!' he shouted and we shot out through the door and ran to where our bicycles lay in readiness. Ringing our bells, we vanished into the darkness, leaving behind us the confused shouts of the boys who had emerged from the hut and were chasing after us in vain pursuit.

Albert Oke at the chapel organ with my grandmother standing just behind him

Chapter 9

Learning to Sing

My last year at primary school was spent in the class of a strict teacher of whom we were all afraid. With her sharp eyes, shrill voice and grey hair plaited tightly in a circle around her head, Miss Smale was the picture of the traditional schoolmarm. Boys and girls sat in pairs in desks drawn up next to each other. The boys in this way were subdued by their own shyness or by the girls' example. Many of us dreaded entering this class because at this stage we had to learn the last of our tables. History lessons seemed to go on for ever and, while I tried to give them my full concentration, I had very little idea of what I was being taught. Singing lessons were taken by the headmaster, Mr. Pulsford, who was also the church organist. When we were in full flow he would prowl amongst us and incline a large ear to each individual in turn. If he heard any of the boys singing tunelessly he would pounce on him and cry, 'Growler!' When he came to me he paused for an unusually long time and when we had finished the song he told me to sing a verse on my own. After I had done so he said, 'I think you should join the choir. I shall speak to your parents.' Later he presented me with *The Chorister's Pocket Book*, inscribed with a kind dedication.

From then onwards Friday evening was choir night. Both my parents were already in the choir and also belonged to the Choral Society (pronounced 'coral' locally), which performed concerts regularly under Mr. Pulsford's baton. I quickly grew to like the atmosphere of the dimly lit church and the degree of informality and freedom to make normal conversation which prevailed, a contrast to the hush required at Sunday services or at Sunday school which I had attended regularly, with only occasional protests, since early childhood. In those days a much larger proportion of the town worshipped publicly on Sundays and one might be asked, 'Are you Church or Chapel?' The father of one family, which had fallen out with the rector, declared defiantly, 'Us be going to Chapel.' My mother had been brought up Chapel, where my grandfather had taught at the Sunday school, but joined the church after she married my father.

Easter was approaching when I first joined the choir and it was rehearsing Stainer's *Crucifixion*. I started going downstairs early each morning to pick up the score and as my parents awoke they heard the strains of 'Fling wide the gates'! Sunday was no longer a day of rest, apart from the extra hour or so in bed. A typical morning would proceed like this – grapefruit followed by boiled eggs, instead of the usual fried bacon and egg, a race for the bathroom during which, at 10.30, the bells would start ringing and I would be the first to leave the house, my heart missing a few beats as the ringing stopped until I remembered that the bell-ringers always took a break. The rest of the family then followed me up the road at various intervals, the last to leave locking up and leaving the key under the doormat. Crime was almost unheard of in Holsworthy at that time as also demonstrated by the fact that my father never removed the car keys after parking when he came home from work. Having arrived at the vestry, I would begin to panic as I searched through the ruffs, freshly starched and goffered, to find one that fitted. Other boys then arrived and, to the accompaniment of bursts of laughter, deliberately put on surplices that were much too big for them. At the last minute two bell-ringers who doubled as choir members entered the vestry and slipped into their vestments just before the arrival of the rector. We then processed up the central aisle, preceded by Mr. Taylor, the cross-bearer, in his red cassock – the rest of us in purple – and his special square-necked surplice, and filed into the choir stalls where the ladies were already sitting.

There were some good female voices in the choir, especially a pair of sisters, the Merrifield sisters – referred to in this context by their maiden names since they had become well known for singing duets before they had married. A daughter of one of them, Janet Parsons, had inherited a beautiful solo voice. We were also fortunate to entertain, as guest soloists, Jack Sargent, a fine baritone from Pyworthy and Arthur Gilbert, a lyrical tenor, who was, among many other things, mayor, captain of the fire brigade and the conductor of the Methodist Choir which regularly performed oratorios including The Messiah. Among the other choir members, the basses provided a solid foundation while the two spirited tenors, Owen Taylor and Wilfred Trace, also later a mayor, completed the harmony.

The quality of singing at the chapel was something of a revelation to me. After the organist had played the introduction of the first hymn, the entire congregation breathed in and, on the first note, everyone started together, contributing to a wonderful sound which immediately filled the whole building. The chapel organist was Albert Oke who, before Arthur Gilbert, had trained the choir for oratorios in which two of my aunts participated. He was in charge of the family business, Oke's. This shop stocked a full range of quality clothes and fabrics in the tradition of Lovell's, which by this time had become Petherick's. A chapel organist for over fifty years, his organ playing displayed not only a high degree of musical ability but the inward calm which also filled his shop, taken over from his brother Fulford who lived in North Road, with an atmosphere of serenity. Another brother, also a talented organist, was Ben, our Santa Claus. He accompanied his wife, yet another fine singer, on the piano at many concerts. After I had sung a solo one day at a chapel service, the much loved Mr. Vanstone, a chapel steward, pressed half a crown into my hand and told me not to let the singing go to my head, 'I'm sure you won't,' he said.

To return to the church, the organist, Mr. Pulsford, played with great expression but he was at times a little erratic. During a hymn he sometimes miscounted the number of verses and, when we came to the end, would plunge straight on into another one, being then obliged to round it off with an improvised coda. This did give the ladies in the choir an excuse to smile and lightened the atmosphere in the church which might otherwise have become too solemn, especially if the service was sung Eucharist rather than matins, the latter being much preferred by my father. The rector stood at the front of the choir stalls for the reading, with a candle-bearer on either side. On one occasion we noticed that there was a smell of burning. One of the candle-bearers had leant too far forward and singed his greased forelock; he turned bright red as a ripple of amusement passed through the choir stalls. An event with which the Rev. Edward Royle may be associated but which has since died out, is the blessing of the crops on Rogation Sunday. After the service in the church, the choir and the congregation would proceed halfway down North Road, led by the cross-bearer, before turning right into a field belonging to Mr. Kivell. Here, after a hymn or two and a prayer, the rector would bless, along with the crops, the resident pony and other animals.

At the end of our service the organist performed a stirring voluntary on the magnificent old organ. It is believed to have been built in 1625 by Renatus Harris, one of the two most prominent organ builders of his generation, for the church of All Saints, Chelsea. A hundred years later it was moved to Bideford Parish Church but in 1865 the parishioners of Holsworthy bought it for 300 pounds; some time after this Wesley is said to have played his famous composition on it. As the voluntary reached its climax I filtered with the rest of the choir out of the vestry to join the last remnants of the congregation who were still making their way towards the church door and we were borne from the church on a great wave of glorious sound into the bright sunlight.

At around lunchtime on Sundays during the summer we would receive a telephone call from my grandmother to ask if we were going to Bude in the afternoon as we usually did. After they had returned from Canada my Aunt Barbara and her family would also be heading in the same direction. I have already described the large wooden beach huts which ran along a sort of natural promenade overlooking the beach at Crooklets.

All of the other huts had grass in front of them but ours had been worn away by heavy use by my grandmother's children and their families. Here we sat on deckchairs and looked out to sea or talked to people walking past, perhaps former residents of Holsworthy down for their annual holiday. Occasionally, as we looked out, a small aeroplane towing a red drogue target would fly steadily in a straight line just above the horizon and we would hear the sound of firing and watch little puffs of smoke appear. Cleave Camp, at Morwenstow just north of Bude, was still used for training anti-aircraft gunners, as it had been during the war. This was before the satellite dishes, which may now be seen on the skyline for many miles around, began to appear on the site of the former military camp. As the tide started to come in we then went down to the beach for a bathe at what has more recently been described as the Bondi Beach of Britain. I remember when Australian lifeguards first arrived in Bude in the early fifties and gave a televised demonstration of a kind of surfing which we had not seen before, standing up on the boards to ride the waves. In 1953 they established the first surf lifesaving club in Britain at Crooklets and loudspeakers were soon being used to warn bathers to stay between the two flags. Before their arrival the beach had been patrolled by a single man in flannels, who stood at the edge of the sea and blew a whistle to attract the attention of anybody who needed a warning. One of these men had lost his life while on duty, having been struck by lightning.

Sometimes during the summer holidays one of my sisters and I would catch the train for Bude for a day on the beach. Whereas I always liked to be well in time, she refused to be hurried and, on one occasion, my heart sank as I saw the train already in the station when we rounded the corner. As I ran on ahead to buy the tickets it started to leave but Mr. Knight, the stationmaster, had seen us coming and dashed out on to the platform to stop it. The driver then waited for us to cross the line and board.

During summer evenings at Upcott I had, since I was very young, helped my father with cutting the lawn by carrying the clippings in a wheelbarrow to the bottom of the back garden, pausing to watch the clouds of gnats circling above my head. My parents continued working outside after I had gone to bed, and, as the light of the setting sun shone brightly through the window, I enjoyed listening to their happy voices, clear in the still air. During the winter, at weekends, I used to take out my father's collection of gramophone records which was stored in the lounge. For whole afternoons I would listen to Elisabeth Schumann, Paul Robeson, Gigli and Caruso. He also had several records of military bands, some of Elgar's *Pomp and Circumstance* marches and a whole set of *La Bohème*.

I had been for some time aware of the fact that I would not enter the top form of the primary school to take the eleven-plus exam since I was to be 'sent away' to board at a prep school in Bude before my tenth birthday. When Miss Smale learnt that I would be leaving at the end of the spring term she surprised me by showing that she did have a kind heart. Aware of the fact that my life was about to change she set me up at a separate desk in the corner of the classroom and gave me paints and paper and a picture of a peacock to copy, telling me that I could take as long as I liked over it. I spent so many hours on every detail, for fear of making a false brush stroke, that I had painted little more than the outline and some of the tail feathers by the end of term but she did not seem to mind at all. I was taken for an interview with the deputy headmaster of the prep school and then came a trip to Exeter to be fitted out with the school uniform. Cherry red cap and blazer, red school tie, school socks with red tops, two types of sweater, grey and white, with broad old-style Eton collars, macintosh and sou'wester (warning of walks to be taken in strong winds and heavy rain), house shoes, slippers, three pairs of pyjamas, dressing gown . . . the list ran over on to a second page.

On my last day at the primary school I felt awkward. I did not know whether to say goodbye or thank you to the teachers and left quietly as usual. As the buses went past the fence at Upcott, taking the country children back to their farms and villages, I sensed that I was about to lose something and that life would never be quite the same again.

Chapter 10

Out on the Prairie

When I was very young my father sometimes took me on his knee after Sunday lunch and told me a story about his life in Canada on the prairie. When it came to the horse-riding bits he jumped me up and down and went 'Gallopy, gallopy, gallopy' as I chased after the Indians. At such times I thought of him as a cowboy. A lot later, when the two of us were sitting in front of the fire on a wintry Saturday afternoon, he suddenly looked up with a shudder and, looking earnestly at me, said, 'Don't you ever go to Canada. It's the nearest to Hell I've ever been!' That was the first of several occasions when he told me of the other side of his life in Canada, and at such times he would give a different account of some of his adventures, colouring them according to his mood. Over the years, as I pieced them together, they became, like his childhood memories, almost as real to me as my own recollections.

It all began after he had read brochures by the Canadian Government, with pictures of endless expanses planted with wheat and barley, which tried to entice people to buy their own land for less than one and six an acre.

Returning to the auctioneer's office in Tring after the war, my father had hated working indoors, especially when the sun was shining. To relieve the boredom he sometimes drew cartoons on the back of the celluloid collar of an elderly clerk seated in front of him without his noticing. Looking through these brochures he dreamt of wide open spaces and of not having to answer to anybody. One of the auctioneer's customers, a wine merchant, told him that his son was emigrating to Canada shortly to join his fiancée whose brother had a farm in the East. My father had already saved enough money for the fare. To this he added money received from the sale of a few sheep which he had been keeping on the Chiltern foothills, and the two men sailed together on the Cunard ship *Ausonia* from Southampton to Quebec in May, 1925.

On arrival they parted company and my father boarded a train for Calgary, a five-day journey. For the first three days he passed through a pleasant landscape of pine forests and lakes but after this there was nothing but prairie, empty but for the odd group of stooks capped with snow and interminable lines of barbed wire. He grew more and more depressed, wondering what he had let himself in for. Calgary was, by then, already a city with some large buildings in the central part but my father quickly became familiar with what were little more than 'cow towns', with compacted earth roads and wooden sidewalks. The buildings, constructed of wood and corrugated iron, gave Calgary much of the appearance of the set of a Western film, without the refinements, and included general stores, places to eat and drink and shops with saddles and chaparejos – chaps – hanging outside the door. People stood about on the sidewalks, leant against wooden rails, or jogged past on horses kicking up the dust. Horse-carts and wagon boxes provided most of the transport. Everybody was aware of the growing popularity of the T Ford but horses, requiring only hay and oats, were cheaper.

My father had arrived with no more than a trunk and a handful of dollars in his pocket. Almost straight away he realised that he had made a mistake in thinking that he would be able to farm land which the Land Registry was offering so cheaply.

'So they *give* you a quarter section (160 acres) for ten pounds?', a man arriving from the East asked somebody in amazement.

'Not exactly,' he was told. 'They bet you 160 acres to ten pounds that you'll starve to death in three years.'

Those who could afford it would do a lot better in parts of eastern Canada where the land was much more expensive but where the boulders had been cleared and the soil was fertile.

In order to survive my father needed to find work. He went to a government agency which sent him to a place called Crossfield to meet an employer. He sat all day at the station but nobody turned up. Towards dusk, a rough old fellow arrived in a wagon and called out, 'Where's this green Englishman who wants a job?'

'That's me!'

'Well, you can come home with me. Can't pay you anything but I can sure teach you farming.'

They travelled for about ten miles out into the prairie behind a team of horses. On the way Old Moore, as the man was called by everybody, tipped the wagon over and he, my father and his trunk were thrown to the ground. The old rancher managed to hold on to the reins and, with remarkable skill, controlled the horses and got the wagon back on the chassis. When they arrived at the ranch he told my father to go on into the shack. My father started in the direction of the best-looking building. 'Not there, that's the barn!' said Old Moore.

Old Moore's wife had left him some years before and food was provided by his granddaughter, a fine rider but an appalling cook and meals and eating habits were very basic. After they had eaten, Old Moore said, 'Well, you'd best get to bed. We get up at five o'clock.' The ranch hands slept in a hollow scooped out of the ground, with a rough shack built over it. It was divided in the middle and in one half Squealey Pete, so-called on account of his whining voice, was already resting. He was a Swede of about six foot two with a pale brown hairless face, pitted as a result of smallpox. He chewed tobacco most of the time and a trickle of juice ran down either side of his mouth, leaving a brown stain like a Chinese moustache. One of the men warned, 'I hope you're not here when Pete's drunk, he goes berserk!' My father looked around the other half where there was a spare bedstead with a split mattress with flock coming out of the seams but no blankets or pillows. 'Where do I sleep, Pete?' he asked. 'There's a bed in there or you can come in here with me if you like.' My father chose the split mattress and his overcoat. Pete was skilful with horses; that year he had been Champion Cowboy of Alberta after winning a competition to control twelve horses with four sets of harrows, each facing in a different direction. But he had no feelings for the animals. When my father was having trouble pushing his way between a pair of half wild horses, Pete picked up a stick four times as thick as a broom handle and forced them apart with a few heavy swipes.

To amuse himself, Old Moore enticed my father to mount a 'bucking bronco', by which he was promptly thrown. In the evening he liked to harness a team of horses to a buckboard and ride out into the prairie to chase coyotes. 'We'll catch him!' he yelled as he caught sight of one and the buckboard rattled over boulders and ditches or crashed its way through brush.

My father endured the ranch for quite some time. There came a point, however, when, after several long days of winnowing, he was near exhaustion. As he threw his last stook of corn into the machine he thought, 'Thank Heaven, tomorrow is the day of rest!' But the next morning he was woken as usual. Unexpectedly, two vets had arrived to castrate some horses. My father was given the job of lying on their heads to keep them still; he soon discovered you had to get out of their way fast as soon as the vet had finished. One afternoon he did have some time on his hands and went for a walk. After a while a reflection of a building appeared in the haze above the horizon so he kept walking towards it and much later arrived at the door of a neat little bungalow. The occupant, amazed that the agents in Calgary had sent my father to work at such a rough set-up as Old Moore's, said he would come over and pick him up the next morning and take him to the nearest railway depot. This he did, and my father caught a train to Lloydminster, where he hoped he would be able to find a more suitable place to work.

He was soon to learn about the hardships endured by the early settlers. While breaking the prairie they might be pitched off their ploughs and dragged several yards along the ground by frightened horses. He met a dogged Yorkshire couple who had built up a ranch on the edge of

Marshall. The wife had given birth to her first baby on the trail where the only drink was water from a 'slough' (pronounced 'slew', meaning a pond or small lake), filtered through muslin. He heard of one man, with only one arm, who had built his own shack and farmed some 700 acres. The nearest doctor might be some forty miles or more away across the prairie. Women who had been brought up in the East often found that they could not adapt to the hard life, which offered few diversions; and, while their husbands might enjoy the shooting and riding, they were breaking their hearts to return to their former homes, most of them knowing they never would.

After a night or two in Lloydminster, without finding employment, my father went on to Hillmond, in Saskatchewan, where the brother of a friend of his in Tring owned a ranch of some 2,500 acres. He stayed there for about six months, sometimes driving cattle for over thirty miles to the railway station at Lloydminster. Once he arrived exhausted in the early hours of the morning and collapsed on the sidewalk, waking later to find people stepping over him.

It was harvest time and two brothers at a small place called Tangleflags offered him three dollars a day to come and work for them. He was receiving no pay where he was and, besides, the brothers were able to offer the inducement of a horn gramophone and a few records including *The Old Hay Wagon* and the Russian national anthem. Starved of music, the neighbouring farmers would ring up one of the brothers, who had a good tenor voice, on the party line and ask him to sing to them; and when a brass band, possibly of German origin, had passed through the area, the farmers and their wives had followed it around like children. The two of them lived in a birch shack which they had built themselves and they kept their butter and other provisions on the end of a string in a hole in the middle of the cabin, covered by a trapdoor. They had become so bored with each other's company that they addressed all their remarks through my father. One night he was sitting alone in the cabin, in the profound silence of the prairie, when he heard the sound of a distant cowbell. At first he took little notice but as the sound grew louder he started to ask himself why this solitary animal was coming steadily closer. The bell stopped ringing just outside and, as the door opened, he leapt to his feet and shouted, 'Get out you old cow!', only to be confronted by one of the brothers, in his left hand the bell which he had picked up off the prairie and brought home.

They had a little thresher and, after completing their own harvest, they took it to the neighbouring farms and helped the other farmers with theirs. Each worker was in charge of a team of two horses pulling a cart boxed in at the sides with hurdles; he loaded it by himself, pitching in the sheaves until it was about three quarters full, and then joined the queue at the thresher, which had to be kept going. The farmers' wives competed for the reputation of being the best cook and the harvesters were well fed.

At night the skies were clear and it was necessary to cover up well. My father slept under a wagon on straw in the barn and often woke up to find rats running all over him. He once owed his life to a horse. The brothers and he had started driving cattle to the railroad one afternoon and the air was not yet free of heel flies, which would cause the cattle to shoot off into the bluff to try to brush them off. He went after one of them to cut it a way out again when his horse stopped short and refused to go any further. As he tried to edge it forward with his heels one of the brothers came up from behind. 'What are you trying to do?' he shouted. 'That's muskeg [quicksand]. If you go in there you'll never come out alive.'

My father became friendly with one of the neighbouring farmers, a diabetic, and offered to help him to take a few loads of wheat into Lloydminster, some forty miles away. They had loaded up the wagons the previous evening in order to make an early start but the frost had frozen the wheels to the prairie overnight. In the morning four horses could not move them; all they managed to do, in trying to move forward, was to break the singletrees – the crossbars to which the horses' collars were attached. Replacements had to be taken from two of the farm implements and, by attaching six horses to each in turn, the wagons were finally freed and they were able to begin their journey. After this delay, they travelled, without stopping, for some twenty miles until

Threshing in Canada in the 1920s

they were able to see the grain elevators on the horizon, but after another hour they seemed no closer. Hoping to make up lost time, they took advice about a new tract being opened from the driver of a wagon coming in the opposite direction but, after dodging the stumps, found that they had to retrace their steps and lost even more time. By now his friend was desperate and, looking up at the horizon with a wild look in his eye, muttered, 'Those *Hell*-evators!' It was so cold that they fixed the reins and walked behind the wagons, to try to warm up a little. My father said that it was a strange experience to see one's legs moving without any feeling in them.

It was now autumn and the grass was drying up and turning brown. The sloughs were beginning to freeze. In winter there would be heavy snow and the brothers would be tying a rope from the shack to the barn twenty yards away to avoid losing their way in the blizzard.

My father had kept in touch with the wine merchant's son and heard that he had not been happy on his brother-in-law's farm in the East. At one point he had gone west to Saskatchewan and stooked 300 acres of wheat by himself. It had taken him five weeks. They both wrote home and each managed to borrow 250 pounds. They decided to travel together to Vancouver where they took over a small dairy ranch at Capilano. Here they went through a similar routine twice a day, rising at four-thirty to milk and feed the cows, then cooling and bottling the milk and loading the horse float. After delivering the milk they returned for breakfast, cleaned out the cowsheds and washed the bottles. Then came a simple lunch followed by a rest before starting milking and bottling again at about three o'clock in the afternoon. They went to bed by eight after a simple meal, often baked beans heated with bully beef. All of this for seven days a week, Sundays being the same as any other day. After a year of this they had only just broken even.

Disillusioned, my father crossed Canada by train and sailed for England.

Chapter 11

To School in Bude

Perhaps it is not surprising that my father wanted me to have a better start in life after his experiences in Canada and the shock, on his return to England, of economic depression in the late twenties. It was with this in mind that he had decided, now that he could afford it with the income generated by his own business, to send me away for a private education, believing it would gain me an entry to employment 'through the front door', as he put it. While I had no desire to live away from my home and the town which I had grown to love, I took on trust his views on the matter. Public schools were not just about elitism or higher academic achievement. While there might well have been inherent advantages in having been a pupil at one of them, there was also a traditional expectation that we would be prepared to take on the responsibilities of leadership without regard to personal risk.

I shall not dwell at great length on my experiences at my prep school, St. Petroc's, in Bude, as for the most part I was not happy there. Some of the teaching was of a very high standard and the headmaster, in particular, dedicated himself to extending our education beyond purely academic subjects, into carpentry, sport and drama. It was he who took nets, produced the school plays for which he adapted the lines, constructed and painted the scenery and lighting and organised pastimes for dull Saturday evenings in winter. But we were heavily drilled and lived under the threat of corporal punishment.

The day began with cold baths. We lined up at the doors of our dormitories with just a towel around our waists and waited for our turn to file into the bathroom where we plunged into the water before taking a salt gargle from a plastic beaker. In winter it was especially cold as the windows were nearly always left open at night. After breakfast we made our beds. Then came assembly followed by morning lessons and morning walk, or, in the summer term, swimming in the open-air pool, filled with sea water, on Summerleaze beach. After lunch, a rest in our dormitories was followed by afternoon lessons and games. If it was raining, instead of games we went on organised 'wet walks' in our wellington boots, macintoshes and sou'westers, tramping in pairs along roads which had become all too familiar and often back across the cliffs. After tea came 'prep' and then we could play cricket in the playroom with a cut-down cricket bat, or in the summer, practise at mock cricket stumps in the playing field. In most subjects we were given weekly tests and, at the end of each week, all of our marks were added up and read out at the Saturday assembly. If they were above a decreed figure we were 'in the red' and, if this was achieved for a certain number of consecutive weeks, we were taken for a 'red tea' at Prince's Café in Bude. Below a certain level we were deemed to be 'in the black' and, if there was no improvement, a beating followed.

We were expected to be hardy and I spent a lot of time shivering. In addition to the fact that we had to endure cold baths, we were not 'cosseted' by being given adequate blankets at night and many of us resorted to putting on clothes over our pyjamas. In early May the order 'socks off' would be circulated and from then on we would wear sandals with bare feet. Shortly after this it would be 'vests off' and, by about mid-term, as I remember, 'blazers off'. In winter we clung to the radiators between lessons and many of us suffered from chilblains. The routine of our lives continued throughout the weekend. After lessons on Saturday mornings we went on organised walks again. Sometimes we went through the edge of the town and I remember feeling cut off from the normal life of the town as local boys called out scornfully, 'Here come the Red Caps!'

On Sunday evenings we were split into two groups and went into the private part of the house to sit on or around sofas and listen as the headmaster and his deputy read to us for an hour. Halfway through, the sweet tin came round and we were each allowed to take two coloured toffees. I remember being totally absorbed by *The White Company* or a Bulldog Drummond story. We all had singing lessons once a week and the music master invited me to join the choir. I also started to have piano and singing lessons which took place at the same time as normal school lessons. One of my teachers would be amused to see my face light up as I raised my hand to ask to leave the class to go to my music lesson. The music room was a hut which stood in the corner of the staff garden. In the winter the music master, Mr. Stanley Oke, would take my hands between his and rub them in the warm air rising from the top of the paraffin heater. 'You're much too thin,' he used to say.

When I joined the school I still had a Devonshire accent which amused some of the older boys, for, although many of them were local, they were mostly the sons of professional men, wealthy business people or rich farmers. After only a few weeks, without my making any conscious effort to change the way I was speaking or even being aware of what was happening, all trace of my accent was lost for ever and I was speaking with the same accent as the rest.

The school had been started over forty years earlier by two Edwardian ladies arriving from Plymouth, where they had met at another prep school. Their surnames were given to the 'houses' into which the school was divided for competitive purposes – Cherrill's and Vivian's. Many of the school's customs and traditions were established in their day – the walk over the cliffs to the woods of Coombe Valley on Ascension Day where we formed gangs and, armed with sticks, fought mock battles and competed to see which group could take most prisoners before relaxing while we all had a cream tea beside the watermill; the 'Dormy Array', on the evening of Sports Day, when counterpanes were hung from the ceilings of the dormitories to form corridors, silver cups and medals were displayed in grottos by candlelight and trays of orangeade and chocolate biscuits were inexhaustible.

One of the two founders of the school, Maud Cherrill, wrote poems when time allowed her to withdraw from her main passion of teaching. We learnt by heart one of them, *St. Petroc's School Song*, which was included in a selection of her poems published posthumously with the title *Padstow Lights*, and begins:

> Sing me a song of a school by the sea,
> On the Cornish coast where the wind blows free . . .

I was briefly taught Greek by her younger sister Phyllis and remember her eyes filling with tears as she gave a farewell talk to school-leavers. An early pupil at the school was Robert Newton, later to become well known as Long John Silver in the 1950 film *Treasure Island*, and one wonders if he first learned to roll his eyes wildly when looking out from the cliffs at Bude towards Lundy Island, off which I believe some of the film was made.

The first boy with whom I became friends was the eldest of three brothers who lived at an ancient manor farm just outside Holsworthy. He used to invite me out to the farm where I first learnt to ride; on my very first visit, as we came out of a wood the three boys dug in their heels and all of the ponies started galloping down the field; I realised at that point that it was simply easier to stay on than to throw myself to the ground, which had been my first instinct! Sometimes I would see my friend when he went hunting, as I often used to follow the Tetcott Hunt on a bicycle. Standing in a gateway one day, I watched a fox scurry past furtively with its head down; the hounds had temporarily lost the scent. Moments later two young women rode up and asked politely if I had seen it. Feeling sorry for the frightened creature, I pointed them in the wrong direction!

I did a lot of cycling on my own in the lanes around Holsworthy and, if my bicycle needed repair, I took it to Mr. Brockington at Derril, a little hamlet on a crossroads near Pyworthy. Born in Birmingham, he had contracted polio at the age of fourteen, which had left him permanently stooped. His father was a toolmaker and, on coming with his family to Derril, had started a repair business in the buildings and yard next to his cottage. This was mostly small repair work on horse-drawn mowers and various other implements, as well as motorcycles. His remarkable son decided to repair bicycles, being easier for him to manage than motorbikes. He carried on in this business for several decades, drawing boys from Holsworthy and many nearby villages on the strength of his reputation. He seemed always happy and smiled and chatted cheerfully as he put my bicycle to rights with his strong arms and long, skilful fingers. A local farmer, in his youth, used to go to Derril on Thursday evenings with two other boys and sit beside the pot-bellied stove in the workshop as Mr. Brockington tinkered and chatted to anybody who brought their bicycles around after work. When Mr. Brockington heard the up-train pass at ten to nine it was 'shut-up time'. On his retirement, his tools went to Ivor Gifford, another memorable Holsworthy centre forward, who has carried on since in the same business for twenty years.

One evening, after returning on my bicycle from a country jaunt, I passed through the Manor Grounds opposite the church where I decided to have a rest. I propped my bicycle up against a rhododendron bush and was looking across the road to the churchyard when I saw the new rector, the Rev. Arthur Warne, and one of his daughters tidying up around the graves. I started thinking immediately about how I might meet her. The chance came eventually towards the end of a Christmas holiday when she and her elder sister invited me along to a Christmas party for the Church Youth Club. Once I had overcome my natural reserve, I began to enjoy myself; I got on well with both of them and we laughed a great deal. I would have liked to have seen more of them but in a few days it was time to go back to school.

During an earlier Christmas holiday I was to sing a solo at a Bude Music Society concert, run by Mr. Oke, at the grand Grenville Hotel. We passed it every Sunday on our way to and from the church the school attended, St. Michael's, beyond the Bude Canal. With its castellated turrets, high walls and little windows, it filled me with terror as I imagined standing to sing before a large audience there. When the night of the concert arrived I was relieved to find that the club met in a room far smaller than I had feared, in the basement of the hotel, and that there was no sign of any of the hotel guests, only a loyal group of pleasant music devotees who filled the modest number of seats. During the first half of the concert the adrenalin had been flowing to such an extent that I felt very tired and I found myself drifting off to sleep as Mr. Oke, a local man who had qualified as a performer as well as a teacher in London and made several BBC broadcasts, played a Beethoven sonata. My turn to sing came some time after the interval and I gave a rendering of *Come unto Him* from *The Messiah*. The audience applauded loudly and another boy then joined me in an encore, a carol. As we drove home in the dark my father kept saying, 'Wasn't that something?', until my mother could stand it no more and snapped, 'Don't keep on about it!'

From then onwards, on arriving home for school holidays, I would find waiting for me at the foot of the stairs, along with my dental appointment, two or three requests to sing solos at various churches, chapels or concert halls in the area. Highlights included singing at a 'Celebrity Concert' with Peter Wallfisch at the Memorial Hall in Holsworthy, which had finally opened, after much hard fund-raising and a degree of opposition from some of those who had returned from fighting in the war and who felt, rightly or wrongly, that some of the money should have gone into their pockets. After I had received a thunderous applause and sung an encore, Peter Wallfisch, father of the now celebrated cellist Raphael, signed my programme and congratulated me with a smile which showed that he understood the audience's reception for a local boy. I also took the boy's part in a performance of *Elijah* by the Bude Choral Society at which the soloists were two of the Linden Singers (well known at the time for appearances on Max Jaffa's television programme) and the baritone Kenwin Barton from Truro in the part of Elijah. In the rehearsal, after I had sung of the appearance of the cloud which signalled an end to the drought, 'Elijah' beamed at me and later encouraged me to consider attending the Truro Cathedral School. At another Bude Music Society concert I performed *Hear My Prayer* with the Morwenna Quartet, a local group comprising

Joan and Arnold Lomax and Vera and Geoffrey Savage. The latter had many BBC engagements and recorded in Bude with the Cornish soprano Cynthia Glover, of international fame. Some of my performances were in a more light-hearted setting. At an evening of entertainments at Milton Damerel, a little play was performed with gusto following which, entirely relaxed after platefuls of sandwiches, jam tarts and cream, cake and trifle, I launched into *Annie Laurie*. All performers received warm applause and, as we drove home in the dark, this rang in our ears and our conversation bubbled with excitement.

One Christmas engagement was to sing a solo during a Nativity play at St. Michael's and I stayed overnight at the home of my music master. Here I met his daughter, who was about two years younger than me. After the performance I sank into bed, feeling cocooned by the soft colours of the wallpaper and the curtains. To my delight she knocked at the door and brought me in a pile of her brother's 'William' books. This was to be the start of a friendship which lasted for some years.

Loading gravel at Wanson Mouth

Chapter 12

Sand and Gravel

In the early years of running the business, my father and his workmen loaded all the gravel by shovel, a back-breaking task. The 'ballast' – the very large stones, for taking to the crusher – and smaller stones, for placing in muddy gateways, were loaded by hand. Sometimes, to hurry the conversation along when taking an order over the phone, my father would say something like, 'The size of your two fists, like you had last time. I'll see to it.' One or two of the men, built of solid muscle, made light of pitching even the heaviest of rocks into the lorry, not bothering to lower the side or back to make the task easier. In time, my father was able to afford a mechanical loader and could spend more time in the office taking phone calls or doing the paperwork.

Most of the men he employed were contented, although one or two would leave, from time to time, to earn more money from contract work. When that was finished they would return and ask for their jobs back. One of the men who never left was not only as strong as an ox but was also one of those gifted mechanics who could diagnose a fault by simply listening to the engine. My father had an easy-going relationship with his men most of the time, although there were occasional lapses of communication, such as the following exchange between my father and another of his drivers.

'I ain't got no ticket book,' he declared.

'Oh, Chris, your grammar!'

'What's up with it?'

'Two negatives make a positive!'

'Come again?'

'If you ain't got no ticket book you must *have* a ticket book.'

'Oh, yes, I must *have* a ticket book!'

During school holidays, if a lorry was passing through Holsworthy to make a delivery, my father would phone to ask if I would like to be picked up. I loved riding at the front of the lorry and it gave me a chance to see more of the countryside. One day we passed a chapel at the bottom of a hill – I believe it was somewhere between Milton Damerel and Shebbear.

'That's Envy,' said Ned the driver.

When we came to the top of the hill he pointed to another one.

'That's Spite,' he said. 'Envy was built first but there was a bit of disagreement and some of 'em went off and built Spite,' he added with an impish grin.

Ned was a conscientious worker and his optimistic nature was sometimes a comfort to my father. He lived near the beach just above the stream and, if he returned from his final delivery of the day with half an hour to spare, he would go down and start heaping up gravel in preparation for the next morning. On occasions when the tide had failed to bring in much fresh gravel for several days and the beach was beginning to look denuded, my father would say, 'I fear we're coming to the end of it, Ned.'

'Don't worry, boss, Davy'll bring it in,' he would reply. His calm nature was never affected by minor details. When his daughter was getting married my father asked him what her new name would be. He replied, 'I dunno, I haven't asked.'

While my father was working in his office one morning a car drew up and a man stepped out and introduced himself as the factory inspector.

'There's no factory here,' said my father.

'You are operating a crushing machine, aren't you?'

'Yes.'

'I'd like to have a look at it.'

Having satisfied himself over the safety aspects of the crusher, he enquired how many men my father employed and asked 'Where are the toilets?'

My father was starting to get irritated. 'Do you see that copse of trees? *That's* them.'

'And where are the washing facilities?'

'There's a stream running straight through the trees at the bottom of the valley.'

The man left saying that he would be making a detailed report but that was the last we ever heard from him.

If I introduce myself today to a farmer within ten or fifteen miles of Holsworthy or Bude, more likely than not he will say that he has bought sand or gravel from my father. Some of them will have been educated at Shebbear College or grammar school but others will have been more relaxed about their schooling. If you had asked them what they were going to do when they grew up they would have replied simply, 'Farming', as if the answer was obvious. In any case, managing the accounts, along with many other responsibilities, was more often than not in the hands of the farmer's wife. Farmers were rarely reluctant to settle their accounts for gravel supplied but some of the more old-fashioned ones put off for as long as possible that irksome business of actually writing and posting off cheques, even after receiving several reminders. Debt collecting was therefore a necessary task but one which my father enjoyed. The farm of one such customer was nestled deep in the countryside at the end of a long private lane. After leaving his car in the farmyard, my father walked into the fields where he found one of the three bachelor brothers, who ran the farm together, on top of a hayrick in the process of thatching.

'You'm prapper strenger,' he said, 'I'm mortal glad to see 'ee. Unfortunately old George and Tom's gone to market.'

My father asked him if he could let him have a cheque.

'Weel, I don't know if I can or no. Tom's the scholard.' He paused.

'No, darn 'ee, now you'm come I ain't going to send 'ee away without it.'

They went into the house and he went off to find the chequebook. Then, sitting astride a chair at the table, he managed with some difficulty to sign his name, passing the cheque to my father to fill in the amount. 'There,' he said. 'If 'tain't no good I'll do 'ee another!'

It was not always this straightforward. He would arrive at another farm with three packets of fruit gums for the children who were always the first to greet him with delighted faces. The farmer would then welcome him warmly and take him into the kitchen, calling out for his wife. She appeared in the doorway with a broad smile while the children took up a new position behind her and peered out from behind her skirts. A glance around the room revealed the usual chaos – a picture on the wall at the same angle as it had been on the last visit a few months earlier, a pile of washing on one of the chairs and the top of the kitchen table covered with newspapers, the remains of breakfast and a tin or two, with flies hovering over everything.

'Now, then, where's the bliddy chick book?'

'Last time I saw it you put it back in the desk.'

It was not to be found in the desk.

'Behind the clock, then.' The chequebook recovered, the farmer sat down, cleared a space, rolled up his sleeve, took a deep breath, paused and, looking up again, asked, 'Mither, where's me pen to?'

As he started to write, the two boys crept up from behind to watch and starting digging each other in the ribs with their elbows.

'Get out, you boys. Look what a bloody old J you've made me do!'

In the end he decided, 'Mither'd better do it!'

The office was situated on the top of the cliff with a single window giving a view over the beach. It was simply furnished with a desk, a comfortable rotating desk chair with a flexible back, a small table and a large squashy armchair which had once sat in the lounge at Upcott until replaced, along with other furniture, by a matching suite. Even in winter, my father could be quite snug with a Primus stove which he kept going all the time and on which he could boil a kettle. On the lined walls he had put up pictures of racehorses – racing, like cricket, being one of his passions. When passing once on a school walk, I amused my headmaster by making a beeline for the familiar chair as the rest of the party paused at the doorway to say hello.

Out of the blue, it was decided that I should take the Common Entrance exam in the spring, a year and a term earlier than I had expected, since I was also to try for a music scholarship to Blundell's School in Tiverton before my voice started to break. My parents had given some thought to my going for an audition at St. Paul's Cathedral School but they thought that I would not like having to sing in the choir at Christmas and Easter instead of coming home. Blundell's had earned a reputation for singing under the inspired direction of Wilfred Hall and the Motet Club had recently represented the country at a UNESCO festival in Brussels. We travelled to Tiverton and I sang some of the songs which Mr. Oke had taught me, accompanied by Mr. Hall on a Steinway piano; by the twinkle in his eye I knew that I had succeeded. Thanks to patient teaching by the deputy headmaster, I did well in my Latin and French exams but my maths result was dreadful. Since I had already been awarded the music scholarship, I was told not to worry and, as I was not due to start until the autumn term, I was allowed to take my maths exams again. After extra tuition, during one session of which my maths master offered me some lychees (not common in those days), which he had bought for me as a special treat, I managed to achieve the pass mark.

Before my time came to leave St. Petroc's, I had, along with a few other boys, been confirmed at St. Michael's Church. The Rev. Walter Prest, later a canon, who had instructed us, was not only kind-hearted but a brilliant classical scholar and a fine organist. The weekly church service was in sung Latin and many of the liturgical passages became a race between vicar and organist, who both had their interpretation of the dynamics. He interpreted a lack of questions in our confirmation classes to a high level of intelligence, whereas, despite listening closely to every word, we had failed to understand much of what he was saying, and for our confirmation gift he offered us the choice of either the Vulgate or the New Testament in Greek.

Although I had not been happy during most of my time at St. Petroc's, there were a few enjoyable moments, especially when playing in away matches against other prep schools like St. Michael's near Barnstaple or Mount House in Tavistock, which provided bangers and mash for tea after football matches. If we had won, we were allowed to shout at the top of our voices on our arrival back in Bude, as we passed the headmaster's house and approached the school. During my last summer term I was especially happy. On Sundays the headmaster would come with two or three of us who had been confirmed to take communion at the early service at St. Michael's and, on the way back, we would have a bathe in the sea. Many Sunday afternoons were spent on a beach north of Bude which we called Earthquake on account of the large cracks in the cliffs. Here we spent peaceful hours digging for fossils in the rocks, fishing in the rock pools with pieces of cotton and bait, building dams across streams running down the sand or swimming in a large pool with an overhanging rock, known as Tunnel Pool.

We looked ahead to our futures at various public schools with a mixture of apprehension and excitement. Many of us had read or seen the film of *Tom Brown's Schooldays* but we felt that, somehow, everything would be all right and that pride in belonging to a great tradition would carry us through any trials arising from schoolboy cruelty which were still being perpetrated in public schools.

If I were to divide my time at Blundell's into phases it would be something like this – two weeks of euphoria as I strode around in a sports jacket and long trousers (even the tallest boys had still been confined to shorts at St. Petroc's); two year's of variably hard schooling in the form of work, sport, duties such as bell-ringing and laying of the dining room table and fagging; two years of an increasing feeling of gloom and confinement to the point of near suffocation and, finally, a year of slightly relaxed tension as rules eased and the end came in sight.

Meanwhile, as I became more embedded in a world within a world, the real one was beginning to change faster than I realised. When I was at St. Petroc's I had not particularly liked *Rock around the Clock* by Bill Haley and His Comets but now I began to enjoy the variety of pre-Beatle hits which we played on a record player in the communal room where I spent much time during my first two years. *What Do You Want to Make Those Eyes at Me for?*, *Stupid Cupid*, *Tutti Frutti*, *Rave On*, *Living Doll*, *Seven Little Girls Sitting in the Back Seat* and *Great Balls of Fire* were among those that dispelled tensions during our free time. A special treat was to be able to buy a new single or perhaps an EP, at the record shop in Tiverton. We had to wear boaters into town unless we went in by bicycle. Having felt very stupid in my boater on my first visit, especially in front of the shop girls, I resolved not to be put in that position again and adopted the usual practice of hurrying into the town on foot, hoping not to meet any masters on the way, and returning wearing a pair of cycle clips, or with the ends of my trousers tucked into my socks, as I came back up the road to the school.

I have already described my feelings of joy and the sense of remoteness which overcame me as I approached Holsworthy by train as a child. To this was now added the sudden relief of travelling and being alone in my compartment, even the whole train, after my close confinement in the constant company of so many other boys. Just over four years after I left school everything was about to change, however, as, first, steam was replaced by diesel, not quite the same, and then the line was closed altogether and an era ended.

Before long, signs of changes which were to have a major impact on the shops of Holsworthy were beginning to appear. Filling stations and corner shops started to give Green Shield stamps. Aunt Clarice, despite some family opposition, decided to go with the trend for fear of losing customers. Then came the first self-service supermarket, an International, and the writing was on the wall for the traditional style of brisk and happy service, the weighing, the putting carefully into bags and the slicing of meat on request which we had experienced

125

at Vivian's and elsewhere. But I am racing ahead and will get back to Blundell's, which was also about to change radically from the way it had been for decades.

Chapter 13

Public School

I had seen Blundell's twice by the time I came to attend, once to try for the music scholarship and a second time to visit the school tailor to be equipped with school uniform. I was, therefore, familiar with the school buildings of darkish red local sandstone and the contrasting houses of red brick on the other side of the road. The school was founded in 1604 by Peter Blundell, one of a succession of prosperous cloth merchants in Tiverton. Among the school's famous pupils were Dr. Frederick Temple, headmaster of Rugby, who later became Archbishop of Canterbury, in 1896, and R. D. Blackmore, author of *Lorna Doone*, who died four years after this; the book begins with a fight in the 'Ironing-box', a triangle of turf in the cobbled area of Old Blundells, which stands near the centre of town.

I have already referred to the sense of duty which we were expected to imbibe at public school in the fifties, along with the acceptance of a form of training which declared itself openly to be designed for a privileged few. Our school motto was *Pro Patria Populoque* and most of us took it very seriously, in different ways. Those who thought that the world of industry was waiting to welcome them for their qualities of leadership were in for a rude shock but there were more than a few who would be prepared to take on responsibilities which would put their lives at risk – for example, by going into the armed services. One of my contemporaries joined the Kenyan police force while another was a war correspondent in the Falklands. In some ways, we were groomed, under an already archaic system, for services to an empire which no longer existed. On the other side of the coin was the underlying barbarity. All in all we lived in a time warp, insulated from the reality of the world at large, and I felt even more cut off from the small town in West Devon to which I felt I belonged. I found the school atmosphere, with its rigid outlook and the unwritten law that we did not show our emotions, totally stifling and I had difficulty in staying on top of things during the next five years, feeling increasingly that I was losing touch with my true identity.

Each house had its own 'traditions', ordeals which gave older boys licence to impose formalised bullying on their juniors. These included various rituals which took place at fixed points in one's school career. For some, these were terrifying and left permanent mental or emotional scars. There was also a 'New Boys' Test', which took place in front of the entire house. One was expected to be able to identify school and house colours as displayed on various caps, blazers, sweaters, and socks, to give the names of all the boys in the school who were entitled to wear them, to know the names of all the boys in one's house, the nicknames of all the schoolmasters and their wives and children, and, of course, to answer questions on the school's history and folklore. Fagging, which was of various kinds, still had some relevance, since it did give one practice in the basics of cleaning, dusting and polishing which most of us have to do at some stage of our lives.

The fact that all this was being paid for by my father made me feel that I should be grateful but it never crossed my mind that he might sometimes worry about whether he would be able to go on being able to afford it. Although I had a scholarship, much of this was whittled away by the tuition fees which he had to pay for the extra music lessons which I was obliged, as a music scholar, to take and, on top of the school fees, there were numerous 'additional expenses'. Apart from concerns over whether 'Davy' would continue to wash ashore sufficient supplies of gravel, the whole future of the business came eventually into question after objections were raised about the possible impact of the removal of gravel on coastal erosion. A panel was set up to make an investigation. A geologist called in by my father gave some contrary views and pointed to the fact that erosion was taking place naturally in several other areas up and down the coast; I had seen this for myself during my days at Earthquake, north of Bude. Many of my father's loyal customers, in conversation with him, made strong expressions of sympathy, but, as a result of the enquiry, my father, from that time, was only allowed to continue the business under licence, granted for specific periods, and he was not to be permitted to sell it on to anyone when he came to retire or, for that matter, to pass it on to me.

CCF training, or 'Corps', was held once a week on Thursday afternoons but we did not have to join until our second term. Mr. Hall took the opportunity to teach me at his home, during those afternoons, the difficult solo part of Vaughan Williams' *Benedicite*, in preparation for a school performance the following term. It was a struggle to start with but I gradually made progress and began to feel more confident. Mr. Hall wrote to Vaughan Williams to invite him to the performance. He replied that this was, as far as he knew, the first time a boy had tackled the part and sent his good wishes; he regretted that he could not come, however, since he was not in good health. He died shortly after this. A week before we were to perform, I developed laryngitis and lost my voice, recovering it only sufficiently to sing in a trio of another work. Mr. Hall was fortunate in being able to obtain the celebrated Jennifer Vyvyan to take over at short notice. On hearing me sing in the trio at the rehearsal, she came across to speak to me. 'Well done,' she said. 'I can see you would have had no trouble at all with the Benedicite.' This was more than a little compensation for not being able to perform it.

Mr. Hall, nicknamed Jazz, bore a facial resemblance to Beethoven, of whom a portrait hung in the room where he taught piano. He had a remarkable talent for developing boys' voices, producing altos from those which had not fully broken and building resonance in newly formed tenors and baritones. Words were as important as sound and, when he conducted us, he mouthed every syllable and his expressive face broke into a grimace if he detected the slightest flaw.

Most of us considered it a great honour to sing in the Motet Club, which performed widely in Devon and made recordings for the BBC. It specialised in religious polyphonic music by such composers as Palestrina and Victoria, but its repertoire also included madrigals and more modern works. Listening now to the music of Byrd on Classic FM brings back to me the almost overwhelming feeling I had of going back in time and of discovering a feeling of devoutness which is rare in the modern world. A BBC recording in which I had a solo part was broadcast during one Christmas holiday and I listened to it with my parents in the lounge at Upcott. No sooner had it finished than the phone rang. Arthur Codd, who had married one of my mother's cousins and had at that time taken over the running of the garage from my grandmother's brother John, came through with his wife to congratulate me. He was a skilful carpenter and, when I was younger, had given me one of my best ever toys, a wooden submarine which fired torpedoes and a battleship which scattered its parts when a target on its side was hit, releasing a spring. The last big engagement in my singing career was a performance of the Christmas version of the *Messiah* in the school chapel, for which I sang all of the soprano and one of the alto parts. I was to finish where I had begun, with Handel's *Come unto Him*, as within the next few months my voice was to break and the one which replaced it was never to be of the same quality.

I was beginning to study harder now for my O levels. One evening, during prep, out of the silence of a dark winter's night, came the cry of a little owl. It thrilled me to the core. I broke off from my studying and started to write:

> The screech, indignant,
> Sudden to fright;
> Unseen, yet heard,
> Is that bird of the night!

I had, by now, completely lost my singing voice but I had found a new outlet for my emotions through words.

Also at about this time I discovered that I could run. Athletics was the main sport in the second half of the spring term. After doing quite well in the annual cross-country race, The Russell (named after the famous sporting parson and former pupil, Jack Russell), which took place during the first half of the term, I found to my surprise that I was looking over my shoulder during the heats for medium-distance races. My singing had probably helped by expanding my lungs and I had grown suddenly taller. In school athletics at the end of term I came home equal first in the mile and in my final year I won it outright. My running achievements resulted in my being taken into mainstream rugby and I later played for the second fifteen. At the Dartmouth naval college I scored the only try, picking up a loose ball and sidestepping the fullback as he lunged forward in a tackle. At the end of a match against Hele's, the school at which my father's friends had once taught, I was applauded off the field, for not giving up right through to the final whistle, by a warm-hearted side to which we lost in very rough weather.

In my earlier years at the school I had been introduced to less formal sports through my friendship with an unusual boy whose father had retired from the Metropolitan Police and taken over the running of a hunt in Cornwall. My friend was on good terms with one of the schoolmasters, a former Welsh international rugby forward, who kept a pack of beagles. We met him one afternoon in the Lowman valley, below the school, where the beagles were in full pursuit of a hare. Suddenly the figure of a boy we recognised came into view and ran between the hare and beagles, crossing the scent. As the schoolmaster, normally an even-tempered man, turned bright red and erupted with strong language, I realised that the boy had done the unforgivable.

The arts were not given major prominence during my spell at the school but it had not always been so. A highlight of my week was the art appreciation class with Mr. Lyons-Wilson, who opened our eyes to the great painters through postcards projected on to a screen in a room which always smelt of his locally made throat lozenges. A very gifted watercolourist himself, he had joined Blundell's in the mid-thirties at the request of a past headmaster, Neville Gorton, who later, as Bishop

131

of Coventry, was to inspire the building of the new cathedral after the heavy bombing of the old one. Both had come from a public school in Yorkshire where Gorton had been assistant chaplain. During Gorton's time at Blundell's, a beautiful stone altar, carved by some of the boys under the direction of Eric Gill, was installed in the school chapel but, when Gorton moved on, it was removed by his successor, who possibly did not appreciate the modern style of the artist. The headmaster who followed Gorton was one of the 'old school'. For example, after a theft had been committed, he ordered every boy to file past him and beat all those who blushed as they met his stare. The altar was eventually rescued from destruction and, thankfully, some fifty years later, was restored and returned to its original place.

During school holidays I had gone on attending church on Sundays and the new rector, the Rev. Arthur Warne, who had originally come from Cornwall, was like a breath of fresh air in church affairs, bringing to them both physical energy and intellectual vigour. He had played football as a schoolboy at county level and was an enthusiastic spectator on the touchline at Upcott Field. His sermons gripped my imagination from start to finish; they were sometimes drawn from his experiences as a chaplain in the Royal Navy during the war, when he endured many months of waiting in intense heat in the Gulf on *HMS Euphrates*, trying to give moral support to men who were tempted to drink excessively in order to make the time pass more easily. On one occasion, he confided to me that he needed to get away from the confines of the rectory to concentrate on writing a book, and he touched on the possibility of staying at our caravan at Widemouth. When he went on to the parish of Colyton from Holsworthy he did, in fact, find time to write a book, entitled *Church and Society in Eighteenth-Century Devon*, for which he received a doctorate and which has become a standard history text.

My best O-level marks were for my weakest subjects thanks to wizardry in the classroom by my maths teacher, a brilliant chess player, and the drive of my science teacher who exhorted us passionately to work harder with the phrase, 'Bloody guts, laddie!', indicating that we needed to put more effort into our work. After taking the exams, I went with a party of fifteen other boys on a four-week cycling expedition organised by the school chaplain. It culminated in our attending the famous passion play which is held in Oberammergau every ten years, in recognition of a vow made by the people there during an epidemic of bubonic plague. We cycled over a thousand miles, including mile upon mile of interminable autobahn, staying in youth hostels. We had three days' rest, however, when we travelled by steamer up the Rhine from Cologne to Rudesheim, near Mainz. On more rural routes, we cycled on well ahead of the chaplain and stopped at roadside inns to drink beer; when he cycled past some twenty minutes later, we would clamber back on to our bicycles and overtake him again in order to repeat the process.

We were grateful to the chaplain for what he did for us at that time, but only as I look back do I appreciate the debt we owe him for giving us an experience which we would always remember. One evening, in the Bavarian Alps, three of us took a wrong turning and arrived at our destination late that night. Our tiredness – we had already cycled for more than ninety miles that day – was countered as we crossed a high plateau, as, every mile or two, a crucifix suddenly loomed out of the evening mist, making us feel that we were experiencing something special, not shared by the rest. The play itself, which lasted some eight hours, was a moving experience; scenes depicting the life of Jesus were interspersed with tableaux portraying a parallel theme from the Old Testament. The theatre accommodated a massive audience and we were a long way from the stage, but in spite of this the strongest and most lasting impression was the sincerity of the players. During our journey home we again travelled for some days on the Rhine and, when we reached Ostend, I knew that the long days of cycling were over. On arriving at Holsworthy Station from Waterloo with my bicycle, I started to cycle through the town, and only as I turned the corner at the top of North Road did I realise that I was on the wrong side of the road!

Back at Blundell's I began to study for A levels. English was among the subjects I had chosen and I was fortunate to be taught by S. H. Burton, well known for his guidebooks on the West Country, especially one on

133

Exmoor. Being introduced by him, during a lesson, to a new set of books containing the poetry of Hardy, Browning, Wordsworth, Keats or Shelley was an occasion never to be forgotten, opening doors to inner worlds which we had never known to exist. My housemaster, who had played rugby for England and cricket for Gloucestershire, was a gentle and fundamentally kind man of quiet, sometimes brooding, temperament who ruled by always keeping something in reserve. One evening after prayers, he gave us a short history of one of the rituals to which I have already referred, but which for me was yet to happen. At the end, he suddenly crashed his fist down on the table and roared, uncharacteristically, 'There shall be no more of them!' – and, indeed, there were no more. Many of the schoolmasters were very caring. My former maths teacher had always taken an interest in me and called on me on several occasions after I had left school, and continued to keep in touch for a long time until I had started to get myself established in life.

By the time I came to leave Blundell's, I had become a house monitor, with my own fags, and had gained colours for both athletics and cross-country; but, despite these outward appearances of moderate success, I felt unfulfilled. On my last day, the school chaplain took me on one side and told me that things would improve when I had had a chance to forget the tensions which had built up in my head during my time there. It was, however, to take a long while for me to find my feet and start to be normal again.

Chapter 14

Passing Years

One morning I rose from my bed early and cycled to Bude. The air was still cold as I walked northwards across the cliffs towards Northcott Mouth in the early sunlight. A skylark burbled high above my head, barely visible in the pale blue mist. Below, the rocks, like wrecked ships turned to stone, thrust their jagged peaks towards me as I looked down and warned me away from the cliff's edge. As the air grew warmer, I sat in a green hollow above Earthquake beach and watched the waves form a crest, tip forward and roll caressingly across the sand. I had become a dreamer and knew that I would achieve nothing unless I lived elsewhere. Shortly afterwards, I met a long-term friend in the surf at Crooklets beach. She told me confidently that she was attending a London hospital to study 'physio' and I felt that she had already moved ahead of me to a stage of development with which I was still unfamiliar.

Ahead for me lay new worlds, several jobs and new friends. During two long years I worked, variously, as a guillotine assistant in a paper factory in Kent, as a library assistant in London's East End (in the footsteps of the dramatist Arnold Wesker of *Chips with Everything* fame), as a dishwasher at a St. Ives hotel and as an assistant master at a prep school. After this, I obtained a place to study English at Exeter University and went on from there to have a career in journalism in 'the essential parts' – as a farmer once described it to me – of the City of London.

My separation from my home town had begun at the age of ten with my attendance at prep school in Bude. My parents continued to live at Upcott until they died and, after I had left school, I was still welcomed, on my visits, by faces which had smiled at me since my early childhood. One of these was Arthur Gilbert, the man of many parts to whom I have already referred and who described Holsworthy to me on one occasion as 'not a bad little old town'. Another was Mr. Matthews, the town crier, who had made the whole town proud when he won the All England competition in this role at Hastings. Then there was Edwin Kivell, a member of the family of local auctioneers and estate agents, who had so generously allowed us to use his farm at the corner of North Road as a playground; he was born in the year 1900 and died in the year 2000. John Oke, who had inherited the agricultural and coal merchants, Thomas Oke and Sons, once the town's biggest employers, waved to me at Upcott, from across the road, as he was mowing his front lawn. As may have become obvious by now, members of Kivell and Oke families, most of whom had risen to some prominence in the town, were nearly always distinguished by the addition of their first name for identification purposes. The same applied to many other local names, of course, like Rowland or Parsons, often followed by such phrases as 'no relation of Frank Rowland, as far as I know'.

Mr. Ken Edwards, son of the man who had bred pigeons for the Signals Corps and now retired from his senior role at Stacey's, the local builders, would dwell with his wife at our fence for a very long chat, and Mr. Paddison's son, now living in Surrey and down for a holiday, would wave with a bright smile like his father's as he went past.

Molly Perkin, who sat behind a glass screen to take the money at the back of her butcher's shop, used to lean forward in a manner reminiscent of her mother and take a great interest in what I was doing and Gwen Jollow, for as long as I could remember, always smiled brightly and waved on her way to and from the telephone exchange in North Road where she was the supervisor. She and her sister also continued the running of the South Western Hotel in Chapel Street after their mother died.

My Aunt Barbara and the rest of her family had lived permanently a little further along North Road from Upcott since her husband, Anthony Hooper, had retired from a distinguished naval career and she would always drop in to see me when I was staying with my parents. He was born in Torpoint but came with his family to live in Holsworthy not long before the war. At the age of seventeen he joined the Fleet Air Arm as an air gunner and became a pilot and an observer. He was later a lieutenant commander on *HMS Glorious* and was mentioned in dispatches when flying over Korea off *HMS Glory*. He ended his career training midshipmen in Canada at the base *HMS Shearwater*, after which his house was named.

Anybody in need of a chat on most fine days would find the retired doctor, Michael Kingdon, known locally as 'Doctor Mike', near his pretty cottage in North Road. He had planted conifers and shrubs, which he tended regularly, on a piece of land just outside the gates to the football field, partly to give pleasure to people passing by and partly in order to make himself available to talk. He was the son of Dr. Owen Kingdon, to whom I have already referred, but many of his ancestors were clergymen.

The association of the Kingdon family with the Holsworthy area goes back a long way. Roger Kingdon appears to have come to the town from Coldridge, north-west of Crediton, around three hundred years ago. He married Judith Cory, from a local family, in 1733 and one of their sons, John, became vicar of Bridgerule and later rector of Pyworthy. At least three of John's sons became local clergymen including Roger, rector of Holsworthy from 1819 until 1857, and John, rector of Whitstone. This John's son, William (great-grandfather to Dr. Michael Kingdon), succeeded him at Whitstone and married Jane, sister of the legendary 'Passon' Hawker of Morwenstow. While their son Robert Hawker Kingdon was still the rector of Whitstone, their grandsons, Claude and Reginald, (uncles to Dr. Michael), were incumbents of Prickwillow (near Ely) and Stepney respectively while another grandson, Frank, was vicar of Bridgerule, where he remained for seventy years, dying two years before reaching his hundredth birthday.

During the course of my work I sometimes came across the odd person who had spent a holiday in the Holsworthy area, including one who held very fond memories of his visit to the town, when on holiday in North Cornwall with his large family, and especially of the friendly atmosphere of Vivian's.

My father continued to run his business but by now he was beginning to tire of red tape, including the paperwork involved in running a regular country dust round for the council. Tax returns were becoming increasingly complicated and fines were payable if his men failed to keep up their logbooks. Petrol and tyre costs were escalating and lorry repairs were becoming more expensive and irksome. Once, after several days of waiting for the delivery of a spare part from Exeter, he was told 'the right part's arrived but it's the wrong number'! He felt, reluctantly, that it was time to retire, but since he was unable to pass on the business, sold the remaining assets for less than a quarter of their former value. Perhaps it would have had to end sooner or later – even 'Davy' needs time to catch up!

In his retirement, he spent much of his time gardening, interspersed with periods of relaxation, watching cricket and horse racing. There was never a shortage of fresh vegetables for meals during the week and to accompany the Sunday joint bought weekly from Perkin's for over fifty years.

My mother attended to the front garden from where she could wave or go down to the fence to chat to passers-by. One day a car drew up outside and a man's head poked out. The driver had stopped to say that, whenever he went past, he always saw at least one flower growing in the garden, at any time of the year, which pleased her a great deal. My mother spent all of her life in Holsworthy. She was for a while president of the Women's Institute and continued to participate in many of the town's activities until she died. She went on producing home-made cakes, buns, biscuits, tarts and pasties and her children, grandchildren and nieces and nephews, with their children, arriving unexpectedly for a sumptuous tea on the best china, would never be disappointed.

Over the years I started, from the outside now, to see changes in the town gradually taking place. Some of the names above the shops disappeared and were replaced by new ones, and the post office moved from the premises it had occupied for over seventy years. Wide's the egg merchants, which before that had been Dickson's prosperous grocery and bakery, was split up into several small shop units and developed into the Church Arcade, with a passage through the middle. This incorporated not only a health shop but a complementary-therapy centre, a beauty salon and, in the cellar below, a fitness studio which all provided services for a large number of people of all ages.

The number and type of stalls at the weekly market declined slightly as it attracted fewer people; there were less people from the country wandering around in a leisurely manner or chatting in groups. I no longer heard the sales patter of a once familiar market trader and the gasps of the crowd as he offered 'not one, not two, but *three* towels' at no extra cost to the first to take up an offer to buy sheets or blankets at a bargain price. On the other hand, farmers on the way to the cattle market still dropped off their wives to shop, and perhaps joined them later for a drink in one of the pubs before they went home together.

Holsworthy thrived towards the end of the nineteenth century as the centre of an agricultural community, benefiting from the arrival of the railway, and its population reached its zenith at over two thousand. Then followed a decline but, in the second half of the last century, it has gradually risen and now tops that level again. Today's population is perhaps more fluid and less structured. From being a town little known in other areas of the country, it is regularly mentioned on regional or local news broadcasts and is visited by ever growing numbers of people. During the foot-and-mouth crisis, which affected the local economy very badly, it was on national television. People are coming to live there from other parts of the country, some attracted by a calmer and healthier way of life.

Along with expansion came an increase in vandalism, although this has diminished due to more police supervision. Crime is no longer unheard of, however, and, were my father alive today, he would probably lock his car. Sadly, the home of the surviving sister of a family which retired to Holsworthy from a local farm, where my friends and I had once been invited to choose freely from their large stamp collection, was burgled several times in her old age. Children probably feel less safe to wander around the town on their own than they did when there were people like Mr. Osborne, who worked for the council after retiring as a lorry driver delivering sheep's fleeces, always around to keep an eye on them. His son has produced pieces of woodcarving, such as a figure of Jesus dragging a crucifix, movingly created from a block of wood his father had used when chopping sticks. This may be seen in Holsworthy Church, although nowadays this, sadly, is locked when not in use. Another of his pieces, an otter, for which he used timber from the original Memorial Hall, is on display in the Visitor Information Centre.

The past has shown that Holsworthy can accommodate influxes of people from elsewhere. During the war many evacuees were taken care of in homes where resources were already stretched. The Somerset Yeomanry, many of whom were billeted in private houses, were the first soldiers to arrive; after them came the Spanish Pioneer Corps. The town absorbed U.S. troops and four hundred Italian prisoners of war, who were allowed to wander freely about the town after Mussolini had been forced to resign. German prisoners later took their place at the camp.

As the town has continued to grow, new buildings have appeared, spreading out especially on the southern and western sides, providing modern comforts for many, including retiring country folk, happy to leave to others the ongoing maintenance of large farmhouses and old cottages. Not all of the new houses are of the quality of the first and subsequent houses built at Glebelands and adjoining roads, for example, but even those of lower quality at least have mains sewers. This was not always the case; my father once asked a fellow choir member why he was looking downhearted as he was leaving the church, and he explained that it had come round to his turn to dig a trench behind his row of cottages when he got home, to deal with this necessity of life.

The shops in the town change according to demand but each can preserve the original Victorian architecture of the premises. Most of the buildings around the square and beyond are tall, reflecting the fact that tithes had to be paid, calculated on the area of the land occupied, and often the best parts of them are to be seen looking upwards, above the level of the signs. The Church Arcade has now gone; the building now houses a friendly computer shop and the health shop has moved to the square. The cellar below, no longer a fitness studio, is now the studio of the Amanda Brook School of Dance which teaches ballet, tap and disco modern to all ages. It is reached by a side entrance to the left of an ornate Victorian doorway, once the entrance to Dickson's, and is the place where wines and spirits were once stored. The Bazaar, occupying the premises which were once the post office, has been so successful that it has expanded sideways to incorporate the former Huntsman Inn, retaining the stained-glass window of a huntsman with his horn. The Original Factory Shop, like the Bazaar, offering a wide range of goods, occupies the place where Whitlock's once stood and, like its predecessor, Somerfield, which has now expanded and moved out of the square, brings business to the centre of the town – seven days a week! Shoes can still be bought where I tried on my first lace-ups and there is still a chemist's looking down through the square, outside which I once stopped to watch a one-man band. Boots, on the other hand, is now the modern HPT Sport and Leisure shop.

Fewer people actually live above their shops now and the atmosphere is undoubtedly different from when many proprietors did so and when businesses were mostly passed on from one generation to the next, each selling its own wares. Ford's, fruiterer and confectioner, has managed to buck the trend and is believed to be the oldest established shop in Holsworthy, remaining in the same family. Oliver's, the saddler's, which stood opposite, is now a dental practice but an example of Mr. Oliver's craftsmanship can be seen in the Holsworthy Museum – one of a set of 'horse boots' especially made to be worn by a dray horse when rolling the wicket for Holsworthy Cricket Club. Other shops contribute to a blend of the traditional and the new. Wroes, one of the branches of the principal store in Bude, which offers quality goods in several departments, stocks ladies' clothes and household linens. HBH Woolacotts, whose main shop is also in Bude, supplies the latest in television, video, hi-fi and other electrical goods. In the same field, Kings, on the other side of the square, has provided a friendly, local service to customers, who have come to know and trust them, over a period of forty years, stretching back to when some of them bought or rented their first television. I remember Kings taking over the premises from Holding's which for two generations had sold quality shoes, at a time when there were at least five shops selling shoes in the town. Coombe's, with its Bude branch and a reputation for long-serving staff, still provides suits for smart occasions. Petherick's, which succeeded Lovell's, where my grandmother worked as a girl, is now a charity shop. Tidball's, which once proudly offered a spectacular display of quality Devon beef, has gone but the cheerful young man who at one time used to deliver our weekly joint by bicycle, facing instant criticism if it was not up to the usual standard, went on to become the owner of Perkin's and has now passed it on to his sons.

As I write, there is still a café, run on traditional lines, in the corner premises where my grandfather once carved joints of meat or, in the separate shop, was happy to take five minutes to sell a bar of chocolate, and a short walk down Chapel Street leads to a successor of Mrs. Blackshaw's hairdressing salon where my mother once took me to stifle as she had her hair permed. The post office, which has now for over forty years occupied the former premises of Cornish's the grocer, has a good selection of books for sale, including those of local interest, in a section called 'The Bookshelf'.

The museum, refurbished and expanded in recent years, preserves links with the past through its exhibits and themed rooms, including a kitchen with its original cobbled floor, copper and fireplace. Its volunteers are making the town's history increasingly available to residents and visitors through books, some privately published, photographs and research material. The museum also manages, on behalf of the town council, photographs and recorded interviews collected under the direction of Peter Bakel, who also compiled books containing many of these photographs and much historical information. Meanwhile, memories are passed on by word of mouth from one generation to the next, which will help the town to retain its identity as it continues to expand.

Chapter 15

The Years Ahead

Has Holsworthy over the years lost something of its distinctive character? Perhaps this is a question to which many of those who have known and lived in the town, for much or all their lives, will have a slightly different answer, according to their own view of what made it the place it is.

Holsworthy has always been essentially a market town and farming is still the pulse that drives the local economy. It has a thriving cattle market, at a time when cattle markets elsewhere have gone, and much of the business activity on the industrial estate is connected with agriculture. But farmers can no longer afford to linger at the cattle market; having sometimes only one person to help them with their work, they hurry back to their farms after delivering their animals and most of the wives are now able to drive and go to the supermarket for their regular shop. The market square has less of a hum of activity than in the days when I used to sit in the window at Elm Tree House and watch the farmers and their wives chatting in groups. On the other hand, the number of stalls is again rising as control of the market has returned to the town council. Walking around I see more than one stall selling good-quality fruit and vegetables, two plant stalls and two stalls selling freshly caught fish. In addition to these there is a good mix of others, as in the past. A new arrival, which has immediately attracted attention, offers a creative variety of breads to those looking for local food products. Will those visiting the market have the same sense of belonging as in former years? I think of an old man wandering along with an expression of delight after buying a tray of peaches, stopping to show them to anyone he knew.

As the town expands, many local people feel that they are becoming outnumbered by 'foreigners'. My father accepted that it would be many years before he would begin to be regarded in the same way as those born locally. Some of those who now arrive set out to criticise, instead of patiently getting to know more about the town; more often than not, they move on again after a couple of years. Perhaps some people will find more of a sense of community in the recreational activities and clubs which the town provides than in the town itself. The town band, which has a lot of local support, brings together people of different ages and the football club in Upcott Field shares a clubhouse with the British Legion, which is stronger than in many other places. The football club looks set to maintain and build on its prestigious past and fields three men's teams, a ladies' team and two youth sides. Cricket is also very strong, again with a good set of younger players coming on.

Wandering down Bodmin Street, one might stop to read a placard on the wall which records a 'house and garden substantially endowed' – this property having been donated for the use of the elderly people of Holsworthy by Mrs. Thirza Coombe Badock on her death in February, 1964. A narrow private passage opens out into a haven of tranquility away from the traffic. Beyond lies another garden, donated for the benefit of young children by Stanley Rowland, local solicitor and one of the driving forces, along with Tom Kivell, brother of Edwin and head partner of Kivell and Sons, behind the creation of the Memorial Hall. In this garden, those qualified to enter may listen to the sound of the Holsworthy church bells, close to where Wesley once did.

Those with leisure to wander around the town to look at the mixture of buildings, old and new, will find, perhaps unexpectedly, the church tower popping up above the rooftops from different angles, as it does on the fringes of Holsworthy. The Memorial Hall, thanks largely to the dedication of a past town councillor, Arthur Wright, another 'foreigner', from Lancashire, who has lived for forty years in or near

Holsworthy, has been fully renovated – transformed might be a better word – for it was in a very sorry state. It took ten years to raise the money and now provides an excellent venue for weddings and many other occasions and functions, with sound and vision facilities, an IT suite, a bar and a café aimed particularly at young people. Its reopening was marked by an 'extravaganza', designed for people of all ages, which attracted some fifteen hundred people. A booklet, *The Holsworthy Town Trail*, available at the information centre, contains many nuggets of local history; and the route is followed not only by visitors but also by local residents and by pupils at the local primary school.

Looking twenty years ahead there are those with a vision of a town twice its present size providing employment for the surrounding villages, and the area still doing what it has always been good at – farming and serving the farming industry. With a proposed new livestock market, it could become one of three major trading centres in Devon and Cornwall. Agriculture would be complemented by tourism. Under the Ruby Country Initiative, the Tarka Trail could be extended from the other side of Hatherleigh, pass over the viaducts at Holsworthy and end in Bude, making it one of the longest trails in the country. Separate walking, cycling and horse-riding paths would run through countryside of outstanding natural beauty, where a return to the planting of spring barley would encourage the revival of the farmland bird population. At the same time, locally produced food would be highlighted.

The cycle trail would pass through Providence Farm, a small farm on the eastern edge of Holsworthy, where Pammy and Ritchie Riggs have shown, despite the scepticism of others, that the organic rearing of livestock can be viable. Other small farms do have the option, if they so wish, of farming organically without having to go through the increasingly difficult process of becoming registered as organic.

Dual carriageways and motorways now make it possible to go to London and back with ease. Cars pass Upcott steadily throughout the day and well into the night during peak holiday periods. Holsworthy is no longer remote.

The church and the White Hart at one end of Fore Street

Conclusion

On a corner near the church, where the earl's house stood in Saxon times, an iron railing runs along the outside of the pavement to prevent pedestrians from stepping out into the road in front of cars and lorries. But for Bessie Cole, my mother's former nursemaid, this was a place for her to lean. One day, on one of my return visits, I watched her as she looked steadily down ancient Fore Street with a smile on her face, in which there was just a hint of irony. I wondered if she could see the ways of the past still being expressed, largely unconsciously, in the present life of Holsworthy.

Whereas the character and the personality of the child were once prepared by degrees for the wider world, modern methods of communication are capable of forcing into our lives a thousand outside influences which may affect us before we are fully ready to absorb them. Walking around today, on the other hand, I meet many a happy and well-mannered child, who, accompanied by either parent or both, says 'Hello!' with an open and friendly smile.

With world population more than doubling since my childhood and expected to increase by half its present level to nearly ten billion by the middle of the twenty-first century, a town with its traditions and sense of community can make us feel that we still matter. Are the days of the small town numbered or will many of these towns be able to absorb new ideas and experiences, while managing to assert their identity as part of a civilisation to which they belong?

Holsworthy raises its church tower with pride and its bells can

still fill the air with a sound which drowns the noise of passing traffic
or an aeroplane flying overhead. In the words of a former churchwarden,
F. J. Sluman, inspired by Wesley's music:

> Our Holsworthy bells ring sweet and clear,
> The glory of God proclaim,
> And summon all folk from far and near
> To bless and adore His name.

Acknowledgements

I am much indebted to the generosity of a large number of people, some of whom are no longer with us, in the writing of this book which has taken place when time and opportunity have permitted over a period of many years. Among those who have provided essential information on Holsworthy are Mr. Des Shadrick, Devon County Councillor (Chairman 2005-2007) and Torridge District Councillor, Mr. Arthur Wright, former Town Councillor (Holsworthy), Mr. Charles Cornish (former Rural District and Urban District Councillor, past portreeve, holder of many other local public offices and author of *A Small Town at War*) and his wife Jill, a former teacher at the Primary School, Mr. Ralph Chapman, Steeplekeeper and Captain of the Tower (Holsworthy Parish Church) and local historian Mr. Bill Millman.

For my chapter on Aston Clinton I was much helped by former Aylesbury Vale District and Parish Councillor and family friend Margaret Lowe while to writer and broadcaster Derek Wilson (author of *Rothschild: A Story of Wealth and Power*) I am indebted for a much greater understanding of the achievements of this remarkable dynasty. He generously gave me leave to refer to this book for some key information.

I should also like to thank Peter Horton (Reference Librarian at the Royal College of Music and author of *Samuel Sebastian Wesley: A Life*) for his invaluable assistance with some details of the composer's life and Jim Bowman, Archivist at the Glenbow Museum, Calgary, for background information on Canada.

Others who have given me considerable assistance with particular parts of my narrative include Mr. and Mrs. A. Blackman, Mr. D. Blackman, Mr. Douglas Penhale, Mr. John Burnard and Mrs. C.M. Dunford (née Warne).

Among those who have helped by answering questions on specific points are Barry and Angela Parrish, Mrs. B. Hooper, Mrs. J. Vickery (née Hooper), Mr. Daryn Bray (PC Plan-IT), Ann Kivell, Celia Sanders, Mr. and Mrs. John Bowden, Mrs. J. Cornish (née Trick), Mr. C. Osborne, Mr. C. Ford, Stuart Smith (Kings), Ivor Gifford (Gifford Cycles), Mrs. P. Riggs (Providence Farm), Amanda Brook (Amanda Brook School of Dance), Mrs. Yvonne Hooper (formerly Meares) of Meridian Health, Mr. Ross Cook of A. W. Bent (Luton), and the Holsworthy Visitor Information Centre.

I should also like to thank Chris Pringle of Spencer Thorn bookshop.

In assembling and checking information on the town I have found the following publications very helpful – *Holsworthy*, by W. I. Leeson Day, *Holsworthy: caught in the lens*, by Shawn Dymond and Janet Mason, *A Small Town at War*, by Charles Cornish, *Snapshots*, by Menor Piper, *Reflections of Holsworthy* and *Holsworthy: The Passing Years* compiled under the direction of Peter Bakel, and the *Holsworthy Town Trail*.